ALWAYS ON

To Michal, Max and Finn for their love and support and to my father, Professor Emeritus Orm Øverland, for lending his lifetime of editing expertise to this project

Always On
Digital Brand Strategy in a Big Data World

Arve Peder Øverland
Partner ID Management, Oslo, Norway

Routledge
Taylor & Francis Group

LONDON AND NEW YORK

First published 2014 by Gower Publishing

2 Park Square, Milton Park, Abingdon, Oxfordshire OX14 4RN
52 Vanderbilt Avenue, New York, NY 10017

Routledge is an imprint of the Taylor & Francis Group, an informa business

First issued in paperback 2019

British Library Cataloguing in Publication Data
A catalogue record for this book is available from the British Library

ISBN 978-1-4724-4779-1 (hbk)
ISBN 978-0-367-88043-0 (pbk)

Library of Congress Cataloging-in-Publication Data
Øverland, Arve Peder.
 Always on : digital brand strategy in a big data world / by Arve Peder Øverland.
  pages cm
 Includes bibliographical references and index.
 ISBN 978-1-4724-4779-1 (hardback) 1. Electronic commerce. 2. Social media. 3. Big data. 4. Strategic planning. 5. Information technology-- Economic aspects. I. Title.
 HF5548.32.O93 2015
 658.8'72--dc23

                                                              2014020511

Contents

v

List of Figures

About the Author

 Arve has been at the forefront of digital marketing since the mid-nineties. He has spent most of his career based in the United States where he led a digital agency working with some of the world's leading companies and brands.

Before joining id.mngmnt, a management consulting firm specializing on customer intelligence, as a partner, Arve served as Digital Practice Director for Hill + Knowlton Strategies Europe, a WPP company. At id.mngmnt Arve heads the digital consulting practice focusing on building result-oriented digital strategies for our clients and develops governance practices that reduce risk and monitor performance.

Arve resides in Aukra, Norway with his wife and two sons.

Introduction

The thought of collecting the many documents and processes I have written into a guideline for companies and organizations seeking insight into the development of digital strategy and the governance of digital systems and programs came after a series of meetings with leaders from very different companies—from start-ups to global enterprises. It became clear to me as I was listening to them describe the symptoms their companies were showing that the quick fix they were hoping for did not exist. There was no pill that would fix the problem—a lifestyle change was needed. But it is hard to prescribe a lifestyle change when the systems and programs that are showing the symptoms of illness are not clearly understood by leadership and when the people set to manage the systems and programs lack the skills to communicate the opportunities and risks involved in a language leaders could translate into business-relevant goals. These leaders possessed business strategies and their organizations were governed, but there was no clear understanding of what a digital strategy and governance is, who owns it, where it lives within their existing business strategies and what the opportunities and risks may be.

This book is about the flow of data and not about the flow of wires. It is about organizations and their existence within this data flow. How to seek opportunity keeping the "led" light green while avoiding threats that bring your indicators to yellow or the dreaded red when all systems fail. The obvious and simple answer is to develop a strong digital strategy and governance structure, but the truth is that there is nothing obvious or simple about doing this. Once you get into the process you will find it much more complex than you imagined and there are large areas where you have little control. This book is written to help guide you through that process.

Where do powerful strategies come from? How do some companies develop strategies that enable them to outperform others regardless of the state of their industry or the economic climate? How does a company get the essentials to work in regard to the company's strategies such as leadership buy-in and follow through on implementations and performance management without being slow, rigid and check box focused? Developing strategies is a tough and sometimes messy business, and getting past PowerPoint presentations to real-life implementation is virtually impossible for some companies before they slide back into business-as-usual. Yet, some companies succeed time and time again. Is it the extra spark of creativity that gets the enthusiasm from management ranks down to the tactical implementers? Is it the internal teams feeling that they are on to something, something great, that could work if we only put our hearts and brains into it, or is it that an organization and the people involved are not afraid of failing, that they have a self-assured sense about them, sense that makes them feel that they can take risks—calculated risks, and that makes the organization feel empowered.

It is probably a combination of the two: creativity that sparks enthusiasm among employees and the self-assured willingness and strength to take risks. In addition, these

2

companies have a good methodology on pilot testing of new initiatives and programs and processes for implementation and performance measurement. This makes them quick and agile in a fast paced technology landscape where customers' habits and expectations move faster than most companies are able to and where disruption from start-ups and new product introductions is the new order of business. Another key item that sets the successful companies apart is their ability to analyze available data in new and productive ways—an area that has been dubbed "big data."[1]

Finally, it comes down to leadership. In this book I come back to this time and time again, because it really cannot be emphasized enough. A company leadership's buy-in and active and ongoing involvement is a vital success factor. Without it a strategy process is almost certain to be added to the huge graveyard of "paper strategies" and never see the light of day.

A formula-driven approach to strategy work might be appealing to many. There is safety in methods, lists and check boxes. This may be the sentiment that drives some to pick up this book. Looking at the table of contents, you could run this as a sequential process—starting with the business case, tightening up the formulations of your value propositions, and covering the bases in finding facts and developing insights that turn into strategies that you implement under strict governance. Great, but for most companies that will take too long and our thought processes are not linear and not everything has equal importance. That said there are underlying elements that are essential for strategy development. You need to know yourself, your market, your customers and the systems and platforms

---

1 Big data is high-volume, high-velocity and high-variety information assets that demand cost-effective, innovative forms of information processing for enhanced insight and decision-making. Source: Gartner, Inc. IT Glossary.

you are developing strategies for, and yes, the strategy team should follow a process. What I am saying is—don't fall in love with the process, fall in love with ideas—then test and analyze the heck out of them.

So what about the scope of the strategic work? The digital ecosystem for most companies is vast and complex and getting a team to put their mind around all the opportunities and risks from the myriad of digital systems and platforms their company possesses is a mind boggling thought. It is often better to look at sections one at a time. However, I am a proponent of a holistic digital strategy. By this I refer to a company's overarching strategies and tying the digital strategy to the company's business strategy. But determining the actual scope must lie with the individual company and be based on insight and priorities.

You don't have to be a digital strategy consultant to see that technology and the integration of data streams are happening at a breakneck pace. Therefore, in a perfect world your digital strategy process should be fast, agile and implemented by stacking pilot tests of prioritized strategies backed by a rigorous performance measurement program. But we don't live in a perfect world. I know this is true because in a perfect world I would work less, have more time with my family and move at will between the ocean and snow packed mountains. In reality we have to deal with corporate politics, problems that are causing revenues to drop, and constant attacks from competitors. This has a tendency to prolong the process and shift our focus mid-stream, and lack of funding can prevent us from testing new programs as thoroughly as we would like. To stay on course and keep focused requires leadership. Success or, more moderately, a good result is all about your people, their engagement and their buy-in.

Many will claim that digital strategy and governance of digital systems and programs should be part of a corporation's business strategy and corporate governance. The word digital should simply be removed. They are right, but there are two important reasons why I believe that the word digital should remain for now:

1. Companies actually do treat digital as a standalone area of expertise that has spread from its early homes of IT and marketing to all corporate areas, and I believe in speaking in the terms of my clients.

2. Corporations have tools and processes to develop and govern business strategies within finance, supply chain, human resources, customer service, communications, etc., but do not have clear processes and tools for developing holistic digital strategies within these areas. Many fail in considering all data sets that affect all business areas in today's increasingly intertwined world. And the word that is used to describe what is missing is—digital.

The use of the term digital strategy in this book is defined within the disciplines of strategic management, marketing strategy and business strategy as opposed to a more IT centric focus. The object is to introduce readers to the digital strategy process and give the reader hands-on tools to implement and governance to run the programs based on these strategies.

This book covers topics such as:

- **The business case**—The organization needs to understand the opportunities, benefits and risks that are the foundation for why they should develop digital strategy and governance.

- **Brand alignment, positioning and value propositions**—In today's plethora of communication surfaces and the non-linear paths customers and other stakeholders follow to seek information, it is more important than ever that a company has its brand toolbox, from visual language to value propositions, in order.

- **Digital strategy**—A digital strategy that drives toward business goals has become a business essential for progressive organizations. The realization is that a corporation cannot navigate properly without a plan and response mechanism for all the transactions that take place every second in the digital realm.[2] Nor can they grasp the advantages inherent in reading the generated data correctly and shaping products, services and communication to meet and exceed their stakeholder's demands without a strategy.

- **Governance**—Digital governance is a relatively new concept as a defined discipline and is still evolving. Digital governance is not just a communications, marketing and IT issue nor only of interest to these business areas. In its broadest sense it is a part of the overall governance of an organization, but with a specific focus on improving the results, management and control of digital systems, platforms and communications and the data they generate for the benefit of all stakeholders.

- **Performance measurement**—A tough challenge faced by managers and business leaders trying to manage digital systems, platforms and services and the data they generate in today's turbulent economy and complex

---

2 Transaction in this context means all exchanges money, information and words.

technical environment is knowing whether your company is on course and being able to predict and anticipate opportunities and threats before it is too late.

- **Implementation roadmap**—The key at this crucial intersection consists of a two-step implementation model. The first step is implementation planning or review of already performed planning and strategy tasks to solidify the teams and the organization for the roll-out. In this stage it is important to have the patience to make sure that nothing has been overlooked or that there is a break in the planned structure. The second is the development of a tactical roadmap that stacks the roll-out into manageable and measurable pilots that can grow into ongoing programs and complete systems through a test, analyze, optimize and scale approach.

- **Communications and change management**—Here I discuss the importance of anchoring the process within the organization from the development of the business case through implementation. But in addition to anchoring and buy-in from management you need an understanding, willingness and—if you can achieve it—excitement throughout the organization.

- **Capability assessment**—In many organizations, top-level management have an unclear view of their digital capability, and find it very difficult to understand the technical and organizational environment upon which they increasingly depend. Often inadequacies only manifest themselves when projects fail, costs spiral, operational systems crash, or service providers fail to deliver the value promised. Reacting after the fact is not how anybody wants to manage their business and besides, it exposes the company to financial and reputational risk.

- **Risk management**—managing risks and exercising proper governance over digital systems and programs is a challenging experience for business managers faced with an overwhelming amount of data, communication-channel proliferation, technical complexity, a dependence on an increasing number of service providers, and limited reliable risk monitoring information.

- **Supplier governance**—Effective governance of suppliers is a key component of digital governance to make sure that risks are managed and value is delivered from the investment in supplier products and services. Most organizations are highly dependent on a limited number of key suppliers, often on multi-year contracts; therefore governance should be focused on those relationships with the greatest risk and investment.

- **Legal and regulatory governance**—The impact of not taking sufficient care of legal or regulatory requirements can be considerable such as loss of reputation, inability to trade, financial penalties and losses, loss of competitive advantage, and loss of opportunity. On the other hand the benefit of complying with regulatory requirements and using legal measures to protect commercial interests can be considerable.

—— 0 ——

Finally, before you embark on the digital strategy journey, keep in mind that the comment you make online will live longer than the platform you make it on. Think fast and build agile solutions that meet your immediate demand. Test, analyze, optimize, and scale your solutions. Being wrong can give you the right answer. Bottom line, or rather top line as that is much of this book's focus, is behind all the consulting speak—this is about selling more and having satisfied customers.

(1) Always On

The concept of Always On was something that came to me on a plane ride home from a consulting gig somewhere in Europe. I don't remember from where. It gets hard to distinguish one trip from another because cities don't get a personality when you travel like that. The hotels become generic. You email while in the taxi or squeeze in a few calls. Have long restaurant dinners with clients and longer meetings the day after. I don't mean to complain. I'm lucky to have met many interesting people from all over the world. I have learned a lot, heard some wonderful stories and some sad ones too. I truly love what I do and enjoy sitting with client teams and listening to them talk about their outlook on the world, their industry, competitors, their business, where they are going, what will get them there and what they think might be stopping or slowing them down. I'm rarely invited if there's not a problem or an opportunity somewhere. Still, I'm always anxious for that last meeting to end. Collapse in the back seat of a taxi and send a text home that I'm on my way. The early evening security line is very different from the morning line. The ties are off. The unlucky ones have telltale signs of the day's lunch on their shirt. The business traveller is tired and starting to relax. The smiles, sneers and comments sit a little looser—especially if Fast Track is moving slower than the regular line, which happens at some airports. With our belts and jackets back on we hurry to get out of the noise from travellers moving about in the large halls of the airport and seek refuge in lounges. We flash our frequent flier badges to get access to wine, a plate of nuts and most importantly a quiet place to sit.

In the lounge I use my last energy to get this day finalized and the next day sorted out. My phone is as worn out as me and appreciates the charge from the outlet next to my seat as much as I appreciate the sip of wine. I send more texts home. What did I miss and what's on the agenda for tomorrow? I email clients to thank them for good sessions and plan next steps. Get colleagues in the loop and set-up debrief meetings and catch up with the news from my Twitter and LinkedIn feeds. Finally, I check up on the most important least important thing—football—the English Premier League and Tottenham Hotspurs—#COYS.

Plane rides for me, specially returning at night, are for reading or watching some TV series on the iPad or just shutting down and relaxing with music through noise cancelling headphones and letting my thoughts wander. And wander they did. On the flight in question I had a "Jerry McGuire" moment—sort of. I didn't write it as a manifesto out of frustration for the company I work for. It wasn't for a client. As I sat there half dreaming and half thinking it just made perfect sense to me, and I had to write it down.

> *Brands live in an 'always on' world. Dare to stand out and drive traffic to your brand. You must gather a crowd to deliver a message. Speak with one identity, but be different. Hold out your hand, encourage engagement and start relationships. Optimize and scale. Listen and analyze big data to protect, amplify and communicate your brand. Align everything in relation to your vision, mission and values. Loyalty is trust. If you don't position your brand someone*

else will do it for you. Your brand is a company asset. Protect its value, but embrace change. To lead you must be different. Brands live or die in the minds of stakeholders. Inspire and start trends. Get results. Revolutionize your industry.

Always on brand. Always on strategy. Always on.

I read through it a couple of times. It sounded pretty good. I put away the laptop and went back into doze mode. Over the next days I kept coming back to it and reading the short text again and again. Not because it was brilliant, but because it contained a lot of the things I have been talking to clients about for years. That brands live in an "always on" world is nothing new and others have said similar things. The same can be said about encouraging engagement and starting relationships with your customers. Every social media expert and CRM marketer talks about those things. That brands live and die in the minds of stakeholders goes all the way back to the brilliant book on positioning by Al Ries and Jack Trout. And so I could go on and break it down word by word. The thing is I still like it. This is how I want my clients to think and be. Why don't I write about how to accomplish it? Brilliant? Self punishment is more like it. Writing a book is a lot more work than hammering down a paragraph as I did on the plane, but I'm glad I did it. It made me think about everything I do and discover new things. I hope it will be valuable to you too.

The concept of the green led light came up about a decade ago when we were working on digital strategy and the re-branding of a fast-growing mid-size company in the technology sector using an earlier version of the process outlined in this book.

The company had been acquired a couple of years earlier by a private equity firm, the founder[1] had served his buy-out period, new leadership was in place and was now positioning the company for rapid growth with an acquisition as the most likely exit scenario.

They were in the battery business when everything was going portable. Problem was that the battery business was the "Rodney Dangerfield" of engineering and could not get any respect. That made it hard to become an integral partner company involved in the shaping of products from research and development and on through beta testing and into production, and not a supplier quoting on a spec from procurement. It is a very typical desire for a business-to-business company to become an indispensable partner and resource of knowledge rather than "just" a supplier. Often this is beneficial to both companies since most R&D teams do not have experts in all areas of product development. If they did we would not be surrounded by so many mediocre product experiences.

This particular company's focus was manufacturing what they defined as mission critical power sources—mostly for the health sector—creating batteries for such devices as portable defibrillators. Needless to say it is vitally important that when you need such a product it actually works. A very important part of a mission critical portable product is the power source.

Our client had the experts—engineers and chemists—that had dedicated their professional life to making the devices

---

[1] The founder took contact a few years later when he was starting a new venture in the portable power industry. He had liked what we had done with his previous company and wanted to work with us on branding his new company and develop an online marketing and communications strategy. That's one of the greatest compliments you can get in this business.

we carry or drive around with last longer between charges. A noble cause and I love meeting people who are incredibly knowledgeable in their areas. I learn new and fascinating things with every project I'm involved in. Our client needed to 'hook-up' their experts with their customer's experts to create a partnership based on knowledge to increase the perceived value of their service and strengthen their client vendor relationships. We needed to build a knowledge-based brand and we needed to do so where engineers increasingly were looking for information—the Internet.

Part of the process of building a knowledge brand in the digital world for this corporation was to create a strong tag line that their target market would associate with the company and its products and a visual that would be remembered and bring positive connotations. The tag line we came up with was *"The power is on"* and the visual was the little green led light. Since they achieved their goal and got gobbled up by a larger entity and the tagline and led light icon is no longer in use I have put it on the cover as an aspiration and warning to companies as they ponder their digital existence in this always on world.

PART I

The Symptoms

We know that for most of our ailments the root lies in how we live our lives, but our common reaction is to just fix it and get on with it. Here are some stories from recent interactions with clients.

$\boxed{2}$ Companies see Challenges in Digital Transformation

"Studying your customers' interactions with your brand can have an enormous impact on your success if you are able to better the customer experience gradually and consistently over time. If you combine this exercise with other available data on your customers and other external factors—could be weather, physical traffic, economic conditions, etc.,—you are actively using big data as part of your business and you are at today's cutting edge of business practices. Using big data as part of your decision process has proven to give companies a competitive advantage and it is a very fascinating emerging field ..." The consultant is so excited about what he saying that he takes off his jacket and hangs it dramatically on the back of his chair, walks over to the whiteboard and grabs the red marker. The men and women around the conference table follow him with their eyes with expressions varying from light amusement and hope to disbelief and disgust. The consultant, done with his dramatic pause, draws a big cloud on the whiteboard, because as we know you can put anything you want in the cloud ... Okay, I'm allowed to poke fun at myself, but let's stop and take a look at this scenario. This is the life of the digital consultant—often talking a year or two ahead of his audience.

What we call digital has rapidly grown from being a website living at the fringes of your marketing team and a customer database at the clutches of IT in the mid-nineties to a network of interacting systems and data sets hooked into the very DNA of your organization. From looking at visitor numbers and page views in the past, your online traffic is now coming to a multitude of systems and platforms with thousands of variable traffic patterns interacting with your brand at different stages of the relationship lifecycle—mostly on platforms you have little to no control over.

Standing in the same conference room fifteen years ago the discussion would have been on the importance of the Internet and the new possibilities of communication. A few years later the discussion could have centered on search engines, CRM software, ecommerce and analytics platforms. In the latter half of the first decade in this century, mobiles and social media were the hot topics. Today, we talk about cloud computing, big data and digital strategy. The goal and our motivation for doing so are solid. We want to give our client a competitive advantage by taking advantage of the greatest and latest, be where their customers are and understand their customers better.

Technology, at least in the abstract, holds a great deal of promise for companies: greater efficiency, improved customer relationships and even new ways of conducting business. But the flip side is the need for both resource investment and near-constant upkeep to yield results. Business leaders feel overwhelmed by and unfamiliar with digital technologies—

therefore the strange expressions in the conference room at my fictive presentation. People react differently when a new set of opportunities and risks is placed on an already full table in front of them.

The MIT Sloan Management Review and Capgemini Consulting conducted a survey of executives and managers in a variety of industries worldwide to gauge their feelings on technology as it related to their businesses.[1] They found that companies faced a variety of challenges in adopting new digital technologies.

Fifty-three percent of respondents said the top cultural barrier to digital transformation was competing priorities. An almost equal number of respondents, 52 percent, said they were stymied by a lack of familiarity with digital technologies. Four in 10 named resistance to new approaches as a barrier. Internal politics and aversion to risk were seen as less prominent obstacles to digital transformation.

The study also concluded that companies faced a challenge in determining what returns a digital overhaul might yield. While 26 percent of respondents said their company had set key performance indicators (KPIs) to measure return on investment (ROI),[2] 57 percent had not, and 17 percent simply did not know.

---

1 The study was released in October 2013.
2 Return on investment (ROI) is the concept of an investment of some resource yielding a benefit to the investor. A high ROI means the investment gains compare favorably to investment cost. As a performance measure, ROI is used to evaluate the efficiency of an investment or to compare the efficiency of a number of different investments.[1] In purely economic terms, it is one way of considering profits in relation to capital invested. Source: Wikipedia.

But those who had considered the challenge of ROI metrics saw a problem in simply identifying the KPIs that would be useful to them. Other major challenges named by respondents included changing the culture to a degree that would allow KPIs to work properly, and the absence of the management skills necessary to see KPIs through.

Clearly the idea of digital transformation within a company is simpler than digging into the often-messy details of such a sea change. But in the digital world, companies need to gird themselves for the effort or risk being left behind.

Back to the "conference room" scenario. We are there for a reason. Sales can have stagnated, customers are aging and new ones not coming in, competitors are taking over, the new product pipeline needs innovation and new ideas, mergers or acquisitions could be on the horizon, the company's reputation is taking a hit in social media and they realized that there was no response process in place. The list of possibilities is almost endless. The company is feeling the symptoms of a deeper ailment—lack of a holistic digital strategy tied to business goals and a governance structure to operate and monitor the strategy. To deal with these symptoms consultants are brought in and a group of people is invited to describe the scenarios. Looking at the research above it is clear that both culturally and regarding work priority many in the room do not want to be there.

So, to move past the many obstacles, real and imagined, the first order of business is:

- Agree on a thesis that describes what lies at the root of the symptoms

- Next steps for dealing with it

- Set goals for the project

- Get buy-in from all stakeholders.

This section, *Symptoms*, describes some "conference room" scenarios I have experienced and what happened afterward.

③ The Website

What we call digital has rapidly grown from being a website to a network of interacting data sets hooked into the very DNA of your organization. Your customer's traffic patterns are in the thousands of variables interacting with your brand at different stages of a relationship lifecycle—mostly on platforms you have little to no control over. The issues and concerns an organization has to deal with include sales, customer service, reputation, employee branding, supply chain and in some cases license to do business due to pressures and demands from governments or customers.

How to analyze big data sets are not what this book is about. Lately, so much has been written about Big Data that you must have a company in Antarctica selling snow to penguins not to have run into a dozen articles or stumbled into a keynote at a tradeshow. This book is about getting an overview of your digital ecosystem, the resources you have overseeing it, and shaping a strategy and governance framework to move forward. This will enable you to make sense of your data and improve your systems. Because data and performance measurement are important parts of digital governance a chapter has been dedicated to this topic later in the book.

From a vendor perspective everyone wants to own a piece of the digital pie. Digital, across the board, is an area where budgets are expanding and companies know they need to execute. Making digital increasingly attractive for consultancies is the constant evolution of technologies and platforms—it keeps on expanding. If you add to this that within many companies their supplier management structure sits within silos, mirroring their own organizational structure, you will in many cases find no clear ownership to a holistic digital strategy and governance internally or externally. Brand marketing, communications, human resources, information technology and other business functions have their own supplier teams operating under separate strategies. These strategies may all be tied to the company's business goals, but not tied to each other, and adding to the misery, not really communicating with each other. And when they do communicate they do so speaking in different corporate languages. Their Key Performance Indicators are not synchronized, and there is no cross team governance and no clear ownership of the digital ecosystem. This is not entirely the company's fault. We as consultants, fighting for our share, are often not helping to bring these teams and strategies together and in some cases I find vendors providing advice in areas where they do not have sufficient expertise.

This was the case with one of the companies I recently sat down with, a very profitable global corporation with significant operations on all continents. Through a recent internal re-organization some functions had been consolidated and—as they had discovered—some digital areas had been left without owners or rather without owners that cared or had the expertise it would take to move it forward. In other words, they had not done a proper resource mapping before allocating ownership or not quite understood what skill sets were needed to properly operate these functions.

Communications and marketing was left virtually without digital expertise after the re-organization, but nevertheless with the ownership of a major part of the company's digital ecosystem. I was invited in because I had run a related consulting project for this team some months earlier. The reason for the invite was that this unit was now feeling a direct pain from a major digital project not going to plan or if it was according to plan they felt the plan could not be right.

The invite I got was rather nebulous. They wanted to discuss hosting. I clarified that I would not be the right person to consult on technical hosting issues, but I was assured that this was about the strategic aspects of hosting and that they needed some general information. That I can do. As it turned out, however, the meeting was not on hosting, but in a world of shared calendars it was as good a meeting subject as any.

I recognized the young man who came to meet me in their large and open reception area from a few earlier meetings where he had not been directly involved in the projects, but present to give the leadership insight into what was going on. He was ambitious and bright and today he was wearing a smile that told me he was anxious to get the meeting started. We entered into one of their fully-equipped conference rooms where lunch was waiting. Both of us carried laptops, but neither of us made motions to open them.

"We have had three vendor teams working on our new website for eighteen months and they are not close to completion. The estimated price tag is approaching five million Euros. What are your thoughts?" he asked and that was the start of a long conversation that had us both push our next meetings that day. His problem was of course only a symptom of the real problem—the lack of a holistic leadership-mandated digital strategy and governance plan. Within this discussion we discussed everything from why are we building a new website to supplier management best practices. We may even have touched on hosting in relation to the benefits of internal versus external hosting and the difference between a cloud solution and a leased managed set of servers at a hosting facility. I did my best to give him actionable advice on his issue at hand, because I believe that such problems must be resolved even if there are greater underlying issues that must be analyzed and fixed.

When considering a major overhaul or rebuild of the main public facing website for a global corporation such as his it is best practice to first build a business case linked to the company's business goals and objectives and its digital governance. He worked for a company where the main concerns are clear communication of the company's point-of-view on some volatile issues, reputation management and brand building toward main stakeholders, being transparent toward the public, and employee branding to ensure retention and acquisition of top talent The business case should clearly identify which goals and objectives the website can have a direct actionable effect on, where it can have a positive or negative effect on reputation, change stakeholder attitude or behavior, identify risks, and quantify opportunity.

I was well aware that they had no digital governance structure in place. That was the main reason they were in the trouble they were in. If they had had digital governance it would have covered the culture, organization, policies and practices that run the site and provided oversight and transparency of all their digital systems, platforms and communications and the data they generate.

However, it was also important for the safekeeping of the company's investment in the new system that the website was clearly defined as an asset, juxtaposed to the hyper-changing environment of the digital world. On the one side the site needed to be robust, secure and function with today's best-practice standards, but on the other side we discussed that the website will have a short lifespan, as did the other websites they had built over the last two decades, due to changing user expectations and the evolution of technological advancement.

Their website-build cycle in recent history was:

- Total rebuild on an overly expensive, hard to use and a hog of a content management system (CMS) platform in 2007.

- Total rebuild of front-end to match user and brand expectations in 2009.

- Total rebuild project initiated in 2012 with planned migration to new version of a hog of a content management system.

It is a knee-jerk reaction from IT teams of large operations that they have to build sites on complex long-running Content Management Systems that they assume will provide support for the next millennium.[1] They do not stop to see that what they have built is out-dated before it is live and that one build process is almost immediately replaced by another—a very expensive cycle. How many sites launched before 2010 had properly considered our multiscreen environment, mobile

---

1 I am now starting to see a change in IT's attitude towards corporate websites where they are arguing for simpler, more agile and less costly systems.

usage patterns and social media to name some of the changes that have happened? That is a three-year lifespan. For most companies it is best to be light and agile with a strong focus on user experience for all stakeholders. Here I am excluding those businesses that are online in nature and possess tailored needs and strong demands on functionality and innovation, but the processes outlined later in this book would still apply.

Brand pride will also play a role in web development—both for internal teams and external vendors. The enterprise website is a showcase for the company and it is a natural desire to deliver a superior product—but also here it is important that your company defines its optimal strategic positioning and what a superior product means in this context:

1. Is it to be known as a wise spender that meets or exceeds best practice for websites in your industry, or

2. Is it to innovate website design and win design prizes?

The two are not mutually exclusive, but achieving both is more likely if the project is approached with the first sentiment in mind.

Another important factor is to place the build and cost structure of anything you build for online communication and interaction in relation to your true needs or your customer's needs for functionality. Are your needs no more complex than a simple site that provides easy-to-find information in a language your customers and stakeholders understand? Many companies today will build this type of site on inexpensive or "free" open source solutions. A cloud-based inexpensive hosting solution will be adequate both when it comes to security and for handling expected traffic. This scenario, of course, is only valid for companies not susceptible to crises that can cause traffic to dramatically increase in a short space of time. If you are a global enterprise in volatile markets you need a more robust solution. The question is how robust does it need to be?

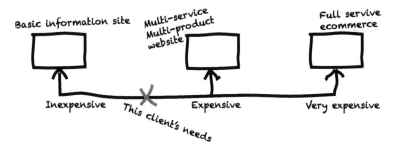

Figure 3.1   Website cost line

In the one extreme you have the basic information site for a small consultancy. A site like this can today be made with small investment in WordPress template and some effort in writing the content. On the other side of the cost spectrum you have the medium to large ecommerce sites with a much higher regulatory demand on security, advanced customer relationship management (CRM)[2] functionality, product and inventory handling, shipping, payment systems, etc. Often the requirements on such a build will demand a combination of custom and licensed software products and in many cases the majority of programming will be handled offshore if

---

2 Customer relationship management (CRM) is a model for managing a company's interactions with current and future customers. It involves using technology to organize, automate, and synchronize sales, marketing, customer service, and technical support. Source: Wikipedia.

your business resides in Western Europe or North America. Between the two extremes we find massive B2B sites with multiple products, services and divisions. The demands on these sites are often such that they are built upon licensed content management solutions that require authorized service providers to make any modification to the code.

My client with the web project problem, although a large enterprise, does not have multiple products, services or divisions. Their needs therefore lie somewhere between the simple site and the massive B2B multi-division structures where a balanced user experience for all key products can be a challenge. They also have a smaller footprint both in regards to functionality and integration and this should be reflected in the overall cost structure from business case to deployment.

Since the company does not have high risk and security requirements such as financial services, the health sector or ecommerce, their build should be made with the realization that it needs to be quickly changeable to new user expectations, adaptable to new technologies or discarded and rebuilt within two to four years after going live. However, they are susceptible to crises and that needs to be accounted for when considering hosting solutions.

We discussed these points in detail in relation to his particular problems and vendor relationships and agreed to revise the business case for the project to quantify opportunities and risks and set a more realistic budget that better matched the functionalities and content needed.

We went through these steps for the revised business case:

1. Pulled the costs associated with front-end and back-end development, hosting, ongoing management and licensing of software over the past six years to get an idea of the investment that had gone into the website

2. Analyzed the data the system had generated and mapped these to business objectives and best practices so ROI could be evaluated

3. Measured against B2B (single service, non-product) best practice:

   a. User experience design
   b. Functionality
   c. Security and hosting
   d. Cost.

5. Measured against the company's specific needs —Business goals

6. Performance measurement—Utilizing existing data to set a baseline and define goals for moving forward

7. Implementation roadmap—Moving forward—what path to follow:

   a. Strategic direction
   b. Content marketing plan
   c. Digital ecosystem playbook.

8. Communications—How to explain the objectives internally and change the culture

9. Capability assessment—Finding out the true current state of digital systems, processes and internal resources' ability to execute and run external suppliers in a mutual beneficial fashion

10. Risk management—What risks exist and how to make sure they are dealt with:

    a. Technical
    b. Reputation
    c. Crisis
    d. Regional concerns.

11. Supplier governance—External parties will play a role and must be included in the governance structure. Some or all of these areas may apply to a varying percentage of the total work load:

    a. Strategic consulting
    b. Data analysis and measurement
    c. Programming and development
    d. Creative direction
    e. Content marketing plan and execution.

12. Legal and regulatory aspects—compliance, privacy, contractual agreements, etc.

The project was given the green light to move forward and the revised business case cut the budget need in half. We will see where it ends.

④ Why are we in Social Media?

Retailers have long had access to vast amounts of transaction data. Every day companies capture information about every product sold at their stores. With every purchase they gain insight into segment behavior to better understand customers' needs and wants if the retailer is set up to study their data in this way. This information can be used to optimize product price points, in-store placement and positioning, and which point-of-sale marketing tactics drive sales.

Adding to the reams of supplier and shop data, retailers have access to an almost overwhelming amount of additional data from the digital ecosystem such as social media interactions and dialog about your brand. Much of it is never looked at or placed in a reporting structure that makes business sense. Social media can provide real-time access to consumer sentiments towards your brand, but when you dive deeper into the qualitative and quantitative unstructured text data you can also find the drivers—the things that drive your customers to purchase and brand loyalty. With a text analysis model companies can use this data to help shape next generations of products and services and work on turning negative sentiments before they cement in the minds of consumers.

Other sets of available data include web and ecommerce analytics. These have long been looked at and reports generated, but a surprising number of companies I have talked to have not actively integrated this data into their steering process at leadership level. Reasons for this are many, but the main problem I encounter is that the reports are not presented in a language the top management understands. Another set of data rarely properly analyzed and used for more than measuring the success of a marketing tactic is the data generated from advertising campaigns. Few companies' structure campaign-generated data so that it creates an ongoing learning platform for future improvement. You might say that it is the media-buying agency's job, but then you are missing out on learnings you have paid for and if you change agency the accumulated learnings get lost. To further add to the data pile many companies conduct primary market research and also subscribe to industry relevant secondary research.

These and other large data sets are known as big data. A study by McKinsey and Massachusetts Institute of Technology released in 2013 showed that companies that inject big data and analytics into their operations outperform their peers by five percent in productivity and six percent in profitability. These and other recent findings have led retailers to search for ways to tap into the potential of data analysis to increase performance and build increased customer value. Defining big data or the relevant data in the data sets available to you in the context of your business objectives is crucial for the development of a sound digital strategy.

Most large-scale retail operations use their transactional data to assure that shelves are filled with the most relevant products for customers shopping at the location where the store is located, and many supplement this with additional data sets. However, sometimes a company lacks crucial data to make vital business decisions. There are holes in the big data pool. This could be due to a lack of measurement or data collecting over time, that the available data is muddled and difficult to analyze or that there is a gap in the data not allowing for conclusions to be drawn between data sets. There are many ways of filling these data gaps. Sometimes it is as easy as modifying the online analysis reports to directly address business goals and KPIs. In other instances you have to construct new programs to properly measure the correlation between online (transactional data[1]) and offline (people shopping in your store) behavior.

One way to measure the relationship between sales and online activities is to conduct geo-targeted test programs as a means to supplement or clarify your data pool. Geo-targeting lets you compare data from different geographic regions where most of the demographic data match and you control the variables. You need good historic data on both regions so you can establish a neutral baseline and be able to consider outside influences that may impact sales such as weather, major sporting events or political elections to name some. Also, competitors' actions could have a great impact on results and must be taken into consideration.

As we have seen repeatedly over the past years, when new platforms reach a certain critical mass companies decide it is probably better to build a presence there than to remain on the outside. Most companies today have a website, Facebook page, LinkedIn profile and a twitter account. With a lack of digital strategy tied to business goals and a holistic

---

1 Transactional data in this context refers to all exchanges that relate to your brand such as clicking on an ad, visiting a campaign or social media page or mentioning you in a blog post.

governance structure your online presences float more or less independently within your company's organization. Often ownership sits with the business unit that grabbed the channel first:

- Human resources own LinkedIn because they set up a profile to post job openings

- Marketing owns Facebook to run campaigns and some have developed content marketing strategies to engage customers

- Media relations sit on the Twitter account and use it as a means to distribute press releases.

I do not intend to blame any of these business units for lack of an overarching brand and business strategy. It is not their job to fully understand new platforms, but they should learn and take them seriously or they will in most instances waste resources barring the occasional lucky strike.

Examples of waste are many:

- Media relation teams using Twitter to post links to corporate press releases without using analytics software with their account to measure performance. Essentially working in the dark.

- Marketing departments running ad-ons to existing campaigns on Facebook, driving customer traffic through ads to application pages just to show them the commercial they are running on TV networks.

- Human resources posting vacant positions on their LinkedIn pages hoping that if you post it they will come. Since they are not marketers you rarely see a content or traffic strategy in such a set-up.

- A website design team is forced to use a brand style guide originally created for print pieces, and the list goes on ...

This was the situation for a retail client with a couple of thousand stores in about a dozen countries. A team of our consultants had been working with their leadership on a totally unrelated matter, but since they were inside they got the question:

"SHOULD WE BE IN SOCIAL MEDIA?"

My colleagues placed the question on my desk and that led to a very interesting project.

Leadership of this particular retail chain had a just case in posing their question. Over the years there had been established, under the retail company's brand, corporate, country, and store-level social media profiles on Facebook, Twitter, YouTube and LinkedIn. There had been an organic growth as opposed to a planned and strategic process. A growing plethora of social media pages and websites existing without strategic direction to grow the brand, but rather exposing the company to possible reputational damage. This mirrors the evolvement of digital eco-systems of many similar corporations, where clarity of brand positioning and voice get reduced and in some cases lead to customer confusion.

For a leadership team focused on increasing store traffic and basket size to make a small margin on the products they stocked, a main factor of concern for the company was the resources spent on maintaining these pages if return was not measurable.

"IS OUR INVESTMENT IN THE DIGITAL SPACE APPROPRIATE TO THE RETURN?"

During our initial discussion I realized that the management team was not against the use of social media; they just had no knowledge of the platforms and could not see how they could benefit their retail business.

Trend reports and case studies are good tools to get an understanding of how something might impact your business, but nothing beats first-hand experience. A task force was established and based on an analysis of available data we outlined a series of tactical initiatives that together would generate a broad set of data and provide the needed learning for the company to answer its own question.

Up to this point country and store level social media pages had been managed and run by the entities that created them—in some cases with a positive impact on their business. Enthusiastic employees had created more engaged customers through dialog in social media. Page managers had increased business through marketing their products and services on different Facebook profile pages.

This in turn raised the following questions:

- If we can generate a positive business impact through social media platforms should we establish a marketing strategy and plan to utilize these tactics throughout the organization?

- What role should social media have within the marketing and communication mix?

- What resources will managing social media require to perform to plan?

- Which efforts should we concentrate on?

- Are there risks and other downsides?

- How should we measure these activities?

- How will this affect our customer service programs?

- Can social media also benefit human resources and other business units?

The task force had members from Communications, Marketing, Customer Service, Human Resources, Sales and Operations and me as a digital strategy consultant. Our mandate was to explore and analyze the questions above.

Because of the company's lack of available data on the effect social media had on their retail operations in countries where they operate, creating and implementing a social media strategy at this time was not attempted nor advised. Instead, the task force held a series of workshops and interview sessions with marketing, sales and operations, customer service, human resources and other units to assess the needs and explore the opportunities of social media within the organization.

These sessions resulted in two main recommendations to the management team:

1. The appointment of a full-time corporate position to oversee and manage all social media channels within the organization.

2. Authorize a series of social media pilots or test programs aiming to test and measure the platforms' performance in relation to existing sales and marketing, customer service and recruitment programs.

These two recommendations were given a green light and the task force completed the social media pilots described below providing the company with valuable data for future decision making.

In order not to interfere with existing business the social media pilots ran as an addition to or completely independent of existing and already planned marketing campaigns, human resources and customer service programs. We decided to run the social media pilots during the summer since this period provided a good mix of campaign opportunities for the retailers. During this period we would test Facebook's effectiveness as a marketing channel as part of the media mix for two planned campaigns. For the rest of the test period we would test two stand-alone campaigns with no relation or interference with other planned summer campaigns.

One of our main objectives for both sets of campaigns, integrated and stand-alone, was to not interfere with the planned creative or media strategies. Our tactics were going to work in addition to the ongoing campaigns without interfering with them. In addition, we did not establish a new measurement methodology or metrics to rate the effectiveness of Facebook. We added the data our tactics generated to their standard campaign measurement data.

The results from the pilots were measured against established key performance indicators. We used the KPIs defined for each pilot to produce our analysis and recommendations. The purpose of this was to generate a good data set into existing processes to be used for further planning by the organization. We emphasized that this project was not about proving or disproving Facebook as a good channel and platform for their purposes, but to provide management with tools to evaluate resource spending in relation to expected results.

Here is an example of one of the integrated campaigns we ran alongside a major new product launch that summer:

> *The country selected for this pilot was Sweden. Marketing had planned and ran an integrated product launch campaign for six weeks during the summer. The planned media purchase, planned and bought by their media agency, reflected their standard media mix with ads on TV, radio, in print and online. The online media plan consisted of display banners, none on Facebook or other social media channels, and paid search through Google. The campaign online destination page resided within their website and contained a product introduction video. This video was also published on YouTube.*

The main objective of the campaign was to explain the value in purchasing a higher-end product in a category where most people shop on price. There was no special offer attached to the campaign. The campaign budget for the total integrated campaign in Sweden was approximately 1 million Euros and was divided and spent as follows:

Google search	€12,000
TV	€520,000
Online (ex Facebook)	€23,000
Print	€25,000
Radio	€160,000
POP	€20,000
Outdoor	€10,000
Production	€230,000

The pilot's test objective was to test the effect of using Facebook as an additional advertising channel in the media mix. The campaign's KPIs were to see if we could see a noticeable difference in purchase behavior between our geographic test area and the rest of the country.

We measured:

- Traffic to the stores

- Sales of promoted product

- Increase in basket size (additional products sold per store visit)

- Online engagement.

To isolate and measure the effect of our Facebook pilot campaign we used a geo-targeted test methodology helped by the geographic and demographic targeting tool within Facebook's advertising platform. Our goal was to analyze the overall campaign results and compare those results with those of the geographic area where we added Facebook advertising. As part of our pilot strategy we used the same campaign creative and messaging for our Facebook campaign as the retailer's advertising agency had created for online display even if that might not be the optimal tone and language for social media. Our goal was to compare apples to apples even if that meant that our results would not show the optimal effect of a Facebook campaign. We selected a geographic area with a total of seven stores fairly isolated in two smaller towns.

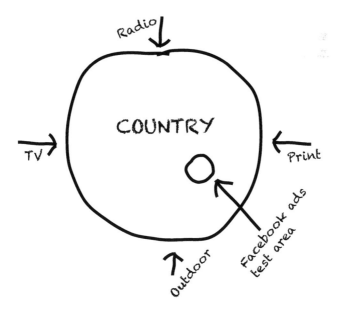

Figure 4.1   Facebook geo test area

The geographic area selected gave us a maximum reach of close to 100,000 unique profiles on Facebook or potential customers. Our only selection criteria beyond where they lived was age—20+ years old. The selection was large enough to provide a valid sample for our test results. We expected our Facebook campaign to reach 80 percent of our target audience or about 80 000 potential customers. Our Facebook media purchase was €13,500 (1.35 percent of a total campaign budget of €1m.) for two million views/impressions, which meant a rate of 20+ views per Facebook profile or potential customer. The ads drove traffic to the store brand's Swedish country page where we were streaming the same video that the other online campaign was pulling viewers to.

Test results online:

- Total views: 2,040,000. The average reach per day: 21,703 unique profiles/customers.

- In total, we received 1475 actions including clicks, comments, shares and likes.

- Of the 1475 actions, 1094 watched the video. Given that the interaction in this case was watching our short film, we expected only one interaction per customers.

    - With a target audience of 75,024 we reached a customer interaction ratio of 1.46 percent. In other words, with this campaign structure and impression density we engaged three of every 200 profiles we reached.

The impact on store traffic was noticeable. The stores in our test area showed an average of 4 percent higher traffic than in the rest of the country. This means that the seven stores that were given a budget boost of 1.35 percent in extra marketing budget on Facebook showed a larger improvement in number of visiting customers than the rest of the stores included in the campaign. Since there were no coupons involved we cannot with certainty track the increase in sales in this area to the Facebook test campaign but the company drew that conclusion based on store performance over time and product mix sold.

The purpose of this test was very clear and targeted. It was to test Facebook's strength, reach and effectiveness as a part of the overall marketing mix during an integrated campaign. We saw that a moderate to small but focused media buy on Facebook was able to get consumers engaged in a ratio of 3-in-200 reached or 1.46 percent. This is very high for an information only campaign. Most campaigns with an actual offer would consider 1 percent a success. Awareness generated through our daily impression reach of one quarter of our potential target audience, increased customer visits in the test area stores by up to 4 percent. The fact that 4 percent of additional traffic was generated by 1.35 percent of the marketing budget is very promising, but we cannot say what effect the total media mix had on this traffic since the effect of other media channels was not measured by the client.

With the pilot we were able to show how engagement on Facebook for the right products can also increase sales. In the future, when our client launches new high engagement products, or has campaigns related to them, they will now include Facebook as part of the integrated marketing mix. With the low cost-to-sales increase in marketing spend shown in this pilot we recommended testing whether these results can be further optimized by increasing the efforts around creating engaging content during the campaign period.

We also suggested testing all media platforms used in an integrated campaign with a similar methodology to what is shown here. This will ensure optimal results from total budget spend.

We ran four additional marketing pilots testing different ways to use Facebook for this particular retail client. For their human resources team we tested recruitment of store and corporate employees using, in turn, Facebook and LinkedIn in two of their markets. We also conducted a pilot that introduced customer service to Facebook and measured for changes in call volumes, resolution times and customer satisfaction. Together the results provided the organization with solid data to guide their digital strategy development and opened their eyes to new ways of thinking. They no longer question why they are present in social media.

Is a Customer Loyal if they're in my Program?

No, they are not. I signed up for a hotel program for the one-time free upgrade offer and never received another benefit even though I stay at the chain frequently on business. I'm a 100K flier, but when I take my family on vacation I shop on cost and stops—they'll never give us an upgrade with an economy ticket anyway. I'm a member in some store programs too because they give money back at the end of year, but if another store has a product I like better or for a better price I'll get it there— loyalty program or not. But you should never use yourself as a single person statistic. What I do or don't do does not really matter in the big picture of a loyalty program. Loyalty programs work. They build preference, conscious or sub-conscious, but not true loyalty. Brand and all the mysteries that go on in our brains when it comes to affection is what builds loyalty. The preference you can build in a customer sector is what matters for loyalty programs, but most programs perform way below optimal, and improvement in preference building, even just some slight percentage points, can have a tremendous impact.

This is not difficult to do, but it requires that you cast a wider strategic net than just the program itself and will most likely involve multiple teams within your organization.

> *In a 'loyalty' program—preference is the immediate objective and loyalty is the goal. In other words 'loyalty' is the 'vision' and 'preference' is the 'mission'.*

Clearly companies are interested in getting more out of their loyalty programs. Even a bad performing program costs money to run. A July 2013 survey[1] on big data adoption found that 64 percent of US executives from financial services and the healthcare industries reported that customer loyalty, CRM and personalization are driving their investments in big data. Customer loyalty is on the agenda everywhere. Customer loyalty plays a big part in CEOs' plans for next year demanding new strategies to stimulate demand and foster customer loyalty from their organizations. A full 82 percent anticipate making changes on this score—and 31 percent have major changes in mind.[2] One obvious measure to work on loyalty is to engage with your customer base and take advantage of the new social media platforms that have established themselves in people's information and communication patterns. But don't make the mistake of jumping in without a strategy.

Most organizations have traditionally used market research, competitive benchmarking and the like to gather customer insights on their brand. But these sources of information can only show how customers behave en masse. That's not the case in the digital arena. Text mining social media sites, blogs, consumer reviews and other such data sources can help an organization find out what individual customers, or rather

---

1   Survey by data and analytics consulting company New Vantage Partners.
2   Source: PwC 16th Annual Global CEO Survey.

clusters of customers think and want and thereby uncover targeted loyalty drivers. Equipped with these insights, you can develop products and services for specific customer segments and craft more personalized marketing messages—as well as enhance your brand. This may explain why three quarters of CEOs surveyed by PwC in 2013 say they're increasing their investments in digital systems and platforms—to collect better and more data for analysis.

A sound digital strategy should seek to find the value of social media engagement and the effect Facebook, Twitter, LinkedIn, Instagram, YouTube or other platforms can have on customer relationship building locally, nationally and globally, depending on where your brand operates. With the growing use of social media, it seems to be one of the few dynamic, cost-effective ways to initiate and maintain connection with a large number of customers and to build a social loyalty program or social CRM as some companies dub it. From what I can see, however, many companies have not yet been able to capitalize on a social media content strategy as an active measurable driver towards defined business goals. Even one of the most common online activities—brand monitoring or listening to your customers or stakeholders—lacks strategic weight because the insights are not analyzed against other relevant data.

Online brand monitoring or "listening" can gain an organization valuable insight and be a necessary part of the performance measurement of your digital strategy. However, structure and consistency are important for these initiatives to generate useful social media insights designed to capture data and answers in response to key questions such as:

- Who is engaging in conversation about our, or our competitors', brands and the products we sell?

- Where are our customers or potential customers engaging?

- What content have they found helpful?

- What are their unmet needs from a product and service perspective?

Armed with answers to such questions companies can refine brand strategy, product selection/development and enhance product information most relevant to their customers. There are many examples of how listening has influenced brand strategies and tactics in retail and non-retail operations. Some relate to better understanding of what customers are saying about their latest campaign, while others glean insights from the language customer's use when talking about their products and services to help craft messaging.

A digital strategy should seek to harness this online engagement towards brand loyalty and increased sales and look at the complete digital ecosystem in which your brand lives. Identify strengths, weaknesses, opportunities and threats with the goal to find the optimal strategy for online to offline traffic drivers at the optimal price point.

One thing is to encourage and advocate online text mining and analysis programs, but in reality most brands with customer loyalty programs are not even doing the most basic individualization of targeting of their communications. Talking "customer loyalty" with the head of sales and marketing for a major airline he told me that when he came onboard he asked who their most frequent flier was. The frequent flier team came back with data that surprised. Their top flier was not a globetrotting business leader, but a guy that commuted back and forth daily on an hour-long domestic flight. Studying the data further he had discovered that the offers and promos the airline had sent their star customer were exclusively for flights to destinations such as Australia, Brazil and Thailand. Good places to go, but if you looked at the data he had never left the country—at least not on their airline. He had enough miles or accumulated points to fly himself and companions across the world, but that was clearly not what he wanted to do. The realization was that the only data the company had used to segment customers and drive individualization was on miles status with no tracking of customers' actions towards the offers so the system would learn from customers' behavior.

The reason I was in the room, however, was not to directly discuss their customer loyalty program or frequent flier program. It was to look at business partner opportunities for their loyalty program. Which partners would help to enhance the customer relationship along the whole journey—literally and otherwise. On the table was partnering with luxury brands in business and first class for a wide range of services and mutually beneficial exposure opportunities, hooking new media brands into lounge and in-flight entertainment and some other very creative ideas. Airlines already have experience with mutually beneficial marketing and sales partnerships. Most airlines offer hotels and rental cars as part of their booking engine. But as we dug deeper into the strong and creative ideas presented we kept coming back to the need to learn more from the existing customer data and pairing that with other research data to uncover what would be most valuable for the customer—which led right back to the customer loyalty program and the low-hanging fruits presented in creating better and more individualistic communications and services.

To start with, frequent flier levels seemed set according to random milestone numbers—25, 50, 75, 100. What if data should show us a distinct change in flying behavior? What if studying leave and return dates revealed a jump in nights away from home at 83K annual miles, but no significant change at 100K—could we then set up something that would make their life easier right away and not wait the painful 17K. What loyalty wouldn't that insight bring?

Another loyalty discussion I had recently was with a CEO of a large co-op with a huge, but shrinking membership base. He wanted to turn that around and find new ways to monetize the member base through partner programs. The main reason the membership was shrinking was that is membership base was aging. That was a serious problem for his large and profitable business—they had lost touch and appeal in younger market segments.

Not all is passed down from father to son or mother to daughter and this company was in that category. To the millennials born 1982 to 2002 they were basically unknown while the same brand had been very important for their parents. Partnering with their advertising agency over the last years they thought they had everything in place to communicate with the youth market; website, Facebook page and a Twitter account, but these places had insignificant traffic numbers as the online traffic generation had been non-existent. Their main communication piece to their member-base was a quarterly member magazine exclusively distributed through the postal service. A magazine is very expensive to produce and distribute—and the only thing growing from that was the returns from bad addresses.

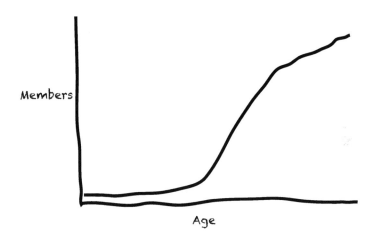

Figure 5.1   Age members

These scenarios are similar in that both companies needed to step back, dig into their data sets, add external research and develop relevant customer intelligence. Not before that is analyzed against business objectives should anything tactical be executed. Strategies should be put in place to address the symptoms their organizations were feeling and properly deal with the opportunities their situations presented.

⑥ Defining a Business Online

In Europe the European Union (EU) has placed severe restriction on the pharmaceutical industry and how they are allowed to market or even talk about their products. There are some exceptions that at least lets a pharmaceutical brand provide some information through a website or social channels, but that is a place few dare to tread. The exceptions include answering a specific question about a particular medicine, factual informative announcements, reference materials without product claims, and human health- and disease-related statements with no direct or indirect reference to the product. While advertising of prescription-only medicines to consumers is strictly prohibited, promoting non-prescription medicines to the public is permitted in some European countries. And for pharmacy retail chains there are no restrictions on their non-medicinal products such as skin, hair care and intimacy products.

That was the background—now to the crux of this chapter:

> *How do you define and position a pharmacy online when you can't show or mention the very thing that defines a pharmacy?*

I was brought in to talk with the CEO and marketing and sales leadership of a major pharmacy retail brand regarding their two-year-old ecommerce operation. Due to the EU directives their online store could only sell products that were not classified as drugs.

The questions at hand as presented to me were:

- Should we invest more in what is now a money losing operation? (said by the CEO)

- Should we invest more in a platform that has not been prioritized and really given a chance? (said by the head of online sales)

- Should we shut the damn thing down and redirect our efforts? (CEO again).

Looking at the spreadsheet this should be a simple question to answer, but there is more to it than how many bottles of sun cream were sold last month through the online store. Pharmacies exist within a commoditized and highly competitive retail market. Could the ecommerce platform support the brand and effect top line results in other ways? Organizations often struggle to justify expenses spent on a company's online eco-system because its total effect is rarely measured. The result of this is insufficient funding of activities resulting in a mediocre presence in many channels—a destructive circle.

For many retailers to quantify the true value of their online eco-system to actual in-store sales they must include and analyze the correlation between "research online—purchase offline" (The ROPO effect). The ROPO effect is the reverse of "showrooming" caused by customers' smartphone's access to online data while the consumer is in the store. In "showrooming" customers go to a store to test a product and purchase it online at a better price. With ROPO, as it might apply to a pharmaceutical retailer, a mother researches waterproof sun protection creams for kids ahead of a beach vacation. Her child has sensitive skin and she wants something that works without having her child's skin break out in a rash or other side effects. When she finds the right product she wants to purchase it in a store locally so she can make sure the smell is not strong or offensive to her.

Failing to properly measure the correlation between online and off-line behavior is like ignoring market trends, and this at a time when smartphone use is skyrocketing and ensuring that ever more research is done online, often at the point-of-sale, and that could be fatal. Bricks and mortar retailers used to metrics such as sales-floor performance must now also measure the role of their website in driving sales in their stores—only then can they get under the skin of their increasingly valuable customers.

To harvest the potential of research online and purchase off-line you must have your products and their descriptions in a context where they will be easily discovered. An online store provides a pharmacy with the incentive and a platform needed to post information on all the products they stock. Many off-the-shelf ecommerce solutions today provide the functionality for product reviews and ratings by customers as well, which will make your product information more attractive to visitors. If you add search engine marketing and optimize your customer facing digital ecosystem to produce traffic to your website you could improve the performance of your in-store sales—in theory, but the assumption would need to be tested. If we would choose to let their online store live and our assumption is right, we can further improve the site by ongoing analysis of visitor behavior and optimize and scale the program to achieve best possible returns.

My discussion with the team at the pharmaceutical retail chain then went from theory to the task at hand—where would we start?

- With all the communication restrictions placed on the European pharmaceutical industry—how do you define a pharmacy online?

- How do you avoid, or should you avoid, your site looking like just another online store?

- How do you further your bricks-and-mortar retail chain brand with your online presence?

- Can you bring what defines you in the mind of the consumer into your online strategy without breaking rules?

- Will it be possible to differentiate your company beyond your brand's visual language?

The answers to these questions are crucial for developing a sound digital strategy, but the answers are not "digital." These are brand related issues and brand questions always come up when you are dealing with customer-facing strategies. That is why I have included a chapter on the symbiotic relationship between brand positioning and value proposition development and digital success.

(7) Data the Great Myth Buster

We have about fifteen thousand possible customers globally. We know where they are and the companies they work for. These people are not online. This is a relationship business.

A sales executive in a global enterprise, in the oil and energy sector, selling complex solutions and services to other large companies told me this in a meeting. He was deadly serious and staring me straight in the eyes. He believed every word. The sales team had been saying this to each other and anyone else who would listen for so long that they all just took it for the truth. I have heard similar statements in dozens of other companies. Corporations have their myths that have become corporate "truths" over the years.

In these initial meetings I do not disagree, I'm there to listen, and I don't have enough data on their specific situation to question their market assessment, but I keep probing, using the data I do have. Usually this seeds enough uncertainty around the statement that someone in management in the room wants the facts—someone with topline responsibilities— "what's our online market opportunity, really?" I know their customers consume industry news and information online, and most likely some on the other side of the table, but that is not going to make a large organization shift their budgets and change the way they have been doing business. We need facts on the table so we agree on conducting an online market opportunity analysis. That is a process where we analyze available data to scope online market size and their behavior. If this initial research reveals a clear opportunity it is often easier to get the organization to go through a needed strategy process. Nothing motivates like a strong upside at the other end of the tunnel.

This company was a major operator in the offshore and maritime industries. The problem was dwindling response and engagement from customers from traditional channels. Their marketing budgets were for a large part focused on the major tradeshows around the world and creating massive, book length, documents on the industry and technology that were printed. Fewer relevant visitors to their booths and shrinking distribution for their book length pieces were damaging their brand. Their brand was a "knowledge brand." That status allowed for premium pricing and trust. Bottom line—this company was dependent on projecting superior knowledge in their areas of expertise. They needed to find their audience. It does not matter how much you talk if nobody is listening. It's like the tired old philosophy question about hearing the tree falling in the forest. As a result, sales had slowed and with a long and complex sales cycle they needed to get more and better leads into the sales funnel.

First we conducted a shallow-dive data analysis looking at all available data from where their customers were not—online. This immediately revealed myth busters—and corporate myths should be busted as they often hamper strategic business development. In this case, where we conducted a quantitative and qualitative data analysis of the status and possibilities within the company and industry's digital ecosystem, we identified several key data points, verified from multiple sources:

- <2.5 million oil, energy and maritime professionals have profile pages on LinkedIn .

- 500,000 of those work in engineering and operations their target audience for lead generation.

- Almost 30,000 companies in their industries have established a profile on the network.

- The company had a larger number of followers on their corporate LinkedIn page than the 15,000 total market size sales were operating with. Even so, this figure was much lower than that of some of their competitors and industry partners.

- The online versions of the top trade publications had close to 1 million visitors to their websites combined every month. Here we knew we were counting people twice or more, but the key was that stakeholders were online searching out industry news and product and service-related information.

- Not only were stakeholders online, but they were also signing up to receive information in their email box at an average of 10 to 15 percent to visitor ratio depending on the trade publication.

- A quarter million people in their target industry sector were active in groups on LinkedIn and more than that had indicated in their profile that they were interested in deal-making contacts. Again, we knew we were counting people more than once, but it showed a strong tendency towards online engagement from their target audience.

Bottom line, this global enterprise's key audiences were online, in large numbers and did not behave any differently from other B2B markets with similarly complex sales cycles that I have looked at. Which brings us to another common corporate myth: "our industry is unique." A statement normally followed by a vague description of why their sales cycle is of stand-alone complexity. Of course it is, to them, since this is the industry they know and hopefully love. People have strong opinions on what they care about, and it is good to see this across the table. Nothing is worse than indifference. Sales people in these large B2B enterprises are in the middle of a battlefield trying to negotiate and land multi-million deals and sometimes you can add a few digits to that. The stakeholders are many and on different continents with a wide variety of informational demands spanning from regulatory to product specific, all of them tough negotiators on cost and delivery time. Yes, it is complex, but not unique. Sales cycles across the board are pretty much the same and if you match complexity across different industries the customer sales cycle is almost identical, with clear commonalities within the personas[1] we draw up to represent the purchase team and influencers.

From a content marketing perspective this means we have patterns to follow. We also know the content formats that go with the pattern from introductory videos to lengthy

---

1 Personas are data built character sketches defined by gender, age, education, geographic location, etc. The approach is to create the persona based on the research and analysis conducted at the start of any strategy process such as customer interviews, ethnographic research, statistical surveys and the company's own user data. Each persona represents a typical member of one customer or stakeholder segment.

technical documents. So the key is to create and update the content with clarity and creativity and to generate relevant traffic to content areas and match the right content with the right stakeholders. What our quick analysis of this industry's online environment showed us was that this company could achieve their marketing goals through a content marketing strategy. We revealed an untapped business potential and the opportunity to attract, retain and strengthen customer relationships through cost effective and targeted online tactics.

There was potential in the online market when it came to strengthening their sales process and stakeholder communications, but their own website told another story. When we looked at product, service and industry relevant search terms and looked at the global volume of monthly searches on those terms we discovered a huge gap between actual and potential traffic. The total search volumes for relevant keyword strings were in the tens of millions showing a very active and information-seeking market. When we cut the keywords down to the most targeted for our client the search volume was cut by approximately 90 percent but that still left us with a significant traffic potential. Their web analytics, however, showed that only an insignificant portion of the available organic traffic reached their site. For those that did enter there was an above industry average bounce rate. The company was missing huge lead generating and content distribution opportunities across the board. Their sales process essentially had no support from their digital ecosystem. No wonder they did not believe in digital tactics and programs. Not only was their site not attracting available traffic, it was not set up to capture leads, and the content was not organized to match stakeholder needs nor the sales cycle.

When we benchmarked their website, country sites and sector sub-sites in a qualitative study in relation to close competitors, they came out slightly below average. Not that achieving an average benchmark in their industry was anything to celebrate. It was difficult to rate the industry as a whole in relation to best B2B online practices as most companies did not meet some of the main features necessary such as clear conversion paths to value-adding content and clear positioning and value propositions by key audience groups. Improving and rebuilding the website would become a central focus in developing their new digital strategy.

I was recently invited to do a workshop on content marketing for another corporate powerhouse. As I was preparing for the workshop I got a call from the organizer asking me not to use the word social media because that would anger some of the participants because it was regarded as not serious. This was 2013. Of course social media was a part of my presentation. They can be important channels in a content-marketing strategy. Nobody got angry. They became interested and wanted more information.

Corporate myths about social media have developed in record time in many organizations. A corporate myth develops as several people within the organization think about and evaluate an issue without adequate data and come up with their own empirical conclusions supported by other likeminded individuals: "My kids are on Facebook, and I'm not, therefore Facebook is for kids." A quick glance at Facebook's own demographic data shows that this is not true, but making people engage with a brand on a social media platform, and a B2B brand at that, is not an easy task. As a matter of fact, it is very hard. It could be easier to just dismiss the channel as the myth builders do.

But for the oil and energy company in question our job was to be myth busters. We also looked qualitatively and quantitatively at their social media presence. By comparison they fared pretty well with most of their competition in social media, but again that did not give any bragging rights, as the level of quality and strategy throughout the industry was poor. They were clearly not tapping into their full potential, as our analysis showed.

At the time of our analysis, Facebook had a strong potential for recruitment and relationship building towards students and young professionals and several large B2B enterprises has done this successfully.[2] They could be more easily and more cost effectively reached on Facebook, a platform they were already engaged in, than through industry channels or their own website. Attracting student traffic, making them care about you and what you do, in a positive way and not as a vocal member of a non-profit organization, is a long-term project. How would you make that conversion on your website? Why would they come back to your site? Building your own tools for connecting with the youth market is not recommended. That is not the business of global B2B giants. It is better to use pre-tailored tools such as Facebook with a built-in geo-targeted traffic.

Many strong B2B brands are using social media and are doing relationship and content marketing successfully. The key is to adopt a tone and content strategy that gels with the target audience and to be always on. Too many marketing

---

2 Approximately six months later LinkedIn launched their pages and programs for universities, students and alumni, which with their power in the professional ranks immediately made them a strong competitor to Facebook in this situation. It will be interesting to see if LinkedIn will be able to become the dominant player in engaging with the younger demographics and combat Facebook here. It also shows the volatile market and times digital strategies live within. It can literally change overnight.

organizations fall into a calendar-based trap and have to make everything follow their campaign cycles. The results are most often a series of failed flurries on social media platforms. This approach often results in further "evidence" for the myth builders that these channels do not work. They do. Simply put, from a marketing angle, the key to building a brand targeting a specific demographic is to connect relevant traffic with relevant content and create an atmosphere for positive engagement. Marketers used to studying online traffic data know that finding the shortest path between targeted traffic and your content is the most cost effective. Social media provide this in many instances and for many stakeholder groups, and for the company we were working with, Facebook provided at the time the most effective option for reaching the coveted millennials contemplating their career options.

Twitter was just as myth laden within this company's walls, and quick witted jokes flourished on how their business was too complex for 140 characters. In my opinion, however, Twitter presented a hyper-effective way to communicate with journalists, political stakeholders and a growing number of industry experts. Therefore we conducted a stakeholder and hash-tag analysis for their market sectors as part of our quick opportunity study. The results were as expected but came as a surprise on their organization. There was an immediate need to revise their media relation strategy to make their point of view visible to journalists as important stories in their realm were developed and debated. We saw a lower degree of urgency in government relations, but relevant activity was growing and many of their identified stakeholders had active profiles. From a knowledge brand perspective the channel started to show signs of meaningful exchanges and information sharing, but this was mostly dominated by consultancies, publications and academia with few brands actively participating with their own knowledge-based information that did not directly relate to their products and services.

As the numbers in our opportunity study demonstrated, LinkedIn presented the strongest and most direct opportunities in social media for this organization. Human resources believed in the platform, but had yet to develop programs beyond posting available positions. The company's sales organization on the other hand was buried in their own myths about digital channels and their industry. Needless to say, nobody had attempted lead generation or knowledge sharing on the platform.

RUNNING PILOT TESTS

The opportunities we uncovered presented some areas that should be tested beyond our assumptions before re-writing budgets and rolling out large programs:

- *Employee branding*: LinkedIn is uniquely positioned in most industries to reach a large talent pool. A proper strategy deployed here should lead to strong talent acquisition in a tough employment market and an opportunity for dialog with candidates who are not yet actively seeking a new job—passive job seekers.

- *Lead generation*: LinkedIn's marketing "engine" for companies gives brands with substantial amounts of company-profile-page followers the opportunity to target stakeholder segments with content they post. We developed a series of strategies from building followers and directing lead generation traffic to campaign pages outside the LinkedIn structure.

- *Trade publications*: The main and traditional channels for communication with their markets had been trade publications and trade shows. Trade publications can be great marketing partners, but since there was no history of tracking results in relation to the marketing spend, the organization possessed no evidence that it actually worked. Which brought us to another myth—"we must be present or we will lose presence in our market." There was a clear lead-generating potential in the main trade publications' online audience size and traffic numbers, but a more thorough evaluation was needed to identify specific publications, tactics to use, and the percentage size of the budget it should take. We included trade publications in our pilots.

- *Search engines*: Our study had found a high volume of relevant searches with a potential to drive significant traffic. We set pilots up to test both organic and paid search engine traffic.

- The pilot program was designed with the ambition to test the efficiency of various online marketing and communications tactics and the channels they ran on. Our metrics were fairly simple: reach, traffic and conversion.

Our client had an important upcoming service release in the spring of 2013 and the content surrounding it was selected as an ideal opportunity to initiate the pilot program. The pilot ran six weeks giving us the amount of data needed to assess the value of each tactic and channel. Our client's new service launch provided a content platform and presented an opportunity to cost-efficiently test the effectiveness of online marketing activities aimed at generating leads and driving relevant traffic to the company's conversion points.

The goal was that the qualitative and quantitative data generated in the pilot test would enable the company to optimize resource allocation and spending, while better gauging expectations and results from marketing activities online. This provided a solid basis for strategic considerations in marketing and communications activities, as well as providing lead acquisition costs for their sales unit to plan around.

The online pilot program exceeded expectations and easily beat the company's previous best case for traffic and conversion. The campaigns succeeded in attracting relevant traffic to the landing page making it the second most visited page next to the homepage on their website for the duration of the pilot and stood for 5.04 percent of all page views. The campaigns saw a 0.57 percent conversion from ads to landing page and 1.93 percent conversion rate from landing page to submission of contact information.

This is how the different channels performed:

- Google AdWords was the channel that delivered the highest traffic volume. Almost nine out of ten visitors to the landing page came from AdWords (88 percent).

- Traffic from LinkedIn had the highest conversion percentage on the landing page, over 10 percent of visitors from LinkedIn converted (submitted their contact information).

- Organic traffic had a relatively low quantity of traffic, but the second best quality (conversion).

- Trade publications drove little traffic to the landing page, but the quality of that traffic was fairly high (6.4 percent conversion).

- The cost of getting a user to the landing page from

    - Google AdWords: $0.79
    - LinkedIn: $3.00
    - Trade publications: $123.00

- The cost of getting a user to enter their contact information to receive content offer:

    - Google AdWords: $50.20
    - LinkedIn: $33.30
    - Trade publications: $1.910.10

- Google AdWords stood for 33 percent of the costs and 50 percent of final conversions.

- LinkedIn stood for 11 percent of the costs and 29 percent of final conversions.

- Trade publications stood for 56 percent of the costs and 2 percent of final conversions.

- Targeting industry professionals delivered a marginally better quality of traffic but was marginally more expensive.

- Their LinkedIn profile had a 66 percent increase in followers.

- In Google AdWords long-tailed keywords drove low traffic volume, but better quality visitors resulting in higher conversion rates. See diagram below for explanation of the long-tail search principle.

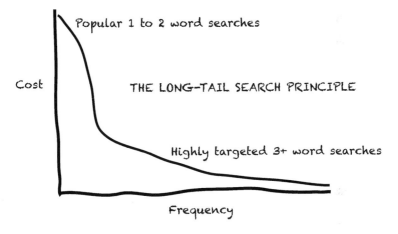

Figure 7.1   Long-Tail

The findings we presented are now used to benchmark performance, channel selection and forecast expected results of similar marketing and communications initiatives and we recommended the following steps for moving forward:

- Identify and create stakeholder personas with clear buying patterns

  - Identify key stakeholders and customer buying patterns
  - Develop clear buying paths for customer groups.

- Clearly position the company's strong brand on multiple digital platforms

  - Define value proposition for individual customer groups
  - Review current brand platform and sales and marketing material
  - Develop customer centric value propositions by customer groups.

- Develop and implement digital lead generation strategy

  - Improve and capitalize on search traffic with a focus on growth markets such as Asia
  - Improve and capitalize on our client's website by creating clear customer conversion paths
  - Strengthen presence/followers on social media
  - Utilize social media and trade publications to drive relevant traffic
  - Capitalize on business opportunities in LinkedIn in particular.

- Analysis and Reporting

  - Set up analysis and reporting structure to ensure that KPIs are met
  - Monthly reporting to analyze behavior, track performance and improve efforts.

- Develop company-wide governance for all digital communication.

- Develop a holistic communication and marketing strategy that encompasses online and offline communication and marketing tactics.

The line items in the list above are part of a standard digital strategy development process that I will go through in the following sections.

(8) The Solution is never the next Gadget

I have now gone through some of the symptoms that I have encountered in my meetings with clients—our website project is out of control; why are we in social media; our loyalty customers are not loyal; our customers don't get what we do online; and our industry is not an online type of industry. The cause of the problems almost always lies deeper and has a much further reach than the symptoms presented. It is always important to address the pain the symptoms cause, because the pain is real, but not to recommend to dig deeper to find the root of the problem will make the pain reoccur and most likely spread throughout the organization. Resist the urge to discuss the latest platform or gadget. You will rarely find the solution there, and just because you work with digital strategy, do not assume that humans will always be replaced by an interface or that new technology will reduce people's need for human interaction—and some things just feel right and will never change.

There is a higher profit margin in leasing less space, serving coffee in paper cups and having people take the coffee with them out the door, but look at the enormous proliferation of coffee shops and chains world-wide that invest in atmosphere and free Wi-Fi. People like to sit down and have a cup of coffee and a conversation. In the conversion between the free Wi-Fi and people spending time with their hot cup of joe there is room for your digital strategies.

A few weeks ago my wife and I attended a friend's record release party. The day after we took our boys down to the record store where they were signing records—all vinyl. That got me thinking. When I grew up I loved records. I loved everything about them. The waiting for an album from a favorite artist. Going down to the record store and listening to it. Buying it and bringing it home. Breaking the seal and placing it on the record player in the living room. Sitting on the couch and studying the cover while listening from the first track on the A-side to the last track on the B-side. Friends would come over with an empty tape. We would sit together and listen while we "pirate" copied the album to my friend's tape.

The arrival of the CD broke the magic. I bought plenty but I never had a relationship with the little shiny disks whether they played music, movies or computer games. They just did not have a personality. The hinges on the cases would always break and leaflets inside were no fun to hold and look through, so when storing and streaming music from my computers became a reality I was quick to transfer my music to hard disks. I never got into "stealing" music from peer-to-peer services such as Napster, but as soon as iTunes made music available online I was a customer.[1] Early on I also tried some of the streaming services, but did not get hooked, so it was mostly iTunes and my ripped CDs feeding my music

---

1   That is not quite true. If an artist or label refuses to make music I want available for purchase through a streaming or downloading service I grab it from somewhere else. I cannot bring myself to purchase a CD that I will just rip to my hard disk and discard.

habit until I pulled out my record player and vinyl collection a few years ago and got hooked on Spotify. In our house now music streams through a Sonos system where we either listen to Spotify or radio stations from around the world or listen to a vinyl record.

My boys were born at the beginning of this millennium. The first time I truly realized how different their perception of the world was than mine was on a trip to Los Angeles, actually to attend another friend's band's reunion concert. We brought our boys and their baby-sitter and decided to make a mini vacation out of it. This was a year or two before the iPhone came out and the rental car did not have a hook up for my iPod something our cars back home had, so we turned on the radio on our way to the hotel—they have some good stations in L.A. My oldest was five or six, still strapped in his booster seat, and singing along to a song he recognized on the radio. When the song was over we heard from the back seat something we were used to hearing "play that song again," but this time I could not. I realized that he had never listened to the radio and had no concept of what it was. I explained to him what radio was. A person sat somewhere playing songs from a list that some other people had selected, so they could sell advertising targeted at a certain demographic in-between every five songs or so. I did not explain it quite that way, but you get the picture. There was complete silence from the back seat as this new information was processed. Then it came— "THAT'S STUPID!" Everything in their world is on-demand: TV programming, movies, games, music, everything. They have never sat down in front of a TV at eight on Thursday to watch a scheduled show.

Back to the story and our visit to the record store. This was the first time my boys were in one. The store was like the stores from my childhood. They only sold vinyl. Most of my boys' music consumption is on YouTube, whether on their iPhones, iPads, lap-tops or a TV set. They have never paid any interest in my vinyl collection. This was different. As soon as they discovered albums from bands they love they were hooked. My boys went from aisle to aisle and pulled up albums from bands and shouted, "look here I found Rage," then The Shins, Arcade Fire, Arctic Monkeys and then my oldest found Foo Fighters. He loves Foo Fighters and David Grohl like only a pre-teen can. Since my wife and I had been out the night before for the release party I had cash in my pocket for tips and such, so I gave him some. He walked to the counter with cash money and bought the record in the same fashion I had decades earlier. In the car home he sat silently with the album clenched in his arms. When we got home he walked straight to the living room, carefully took off the wrapping, asked me how to operate the record player, put it on, turned up the volume, sat in the sofa studying the cover and listened to the album from the first track on side A to the last on side B.

You can decide if this story of digital disruption and digital disruption in reverse has any relevance to your digital strategy and governance project, but what I want to emphasize before we get into the development and process side of things—never disregard the human side. Some things we just do.

PART II

The Business Case

(9) Understanding the Need

If something is going to receive funding you need a business case. So to build consensus and get the green light for digital strategy development in your organization this is where you start: by making leadership understand the need—risks and opportunities clearly described in a few brilliant pages. Companies are not blind, deaf and stupid. They are living vital organizations full of smart people. However, most organizations have a shortage of digital talent in important business units such as customer service, human resources and sales. So in most cases, companies can see the problems and feel the pain of the symptoms of failure within their digital ecosystem, but they don't properly understand them so they can find the root of the problem. The result is often Band-Aid fixes or knee-jerk decisions that are not rooted in business goals but in an immediate desire to minimize pain. For a company's digital ecosystem, as with the human body, the true fix often lies in a lifestyle change—a new strategy for life.

Most companies are not ready to change their ways—ever. For a person to change lifestyle there must be an understanding or a sense that there is something wrong that goes deeper than just the pain in the now. There must be a vision for the future. The same goes for companies.

$500, fully subsidized with a plan?!... That is the most expensive phone in the world, and it doesn't appeal to business customers because it doesn't have a keyboard.

Steve Ballmer, CEO Microsoft, on the iPhone in 2007

The pain was there. Ballmer is a famously competitive person and Apple had beaten them to market with a smart phone. I'm sure that caused him and the company some pain. The problem was a lack of vision for the future. He failed to see what consumers were willing to pay and what functions they were willing to live without, or were actually happy to get rid of—a physical keyboard. I don't mean to put down Mr Ballmer; we all make mistakes. He just happened to make this one when he was still head of one of the world's largest corporations and the main competitor of Apple in a market about to take a huge technological and cultural shift.

—— 0 ——

Not all companies need to completely change their lifestyle when adopting a holistic digital strategy, but at the very least there will be process and resource changes and a need for investment. With the diversified ownership of the digital ecosystem it is not always easy for management to connect the dots and see the business case for a holistic digital strategy and developing a governance framework for your digital systems and programs. That is no excuse and action needs to be taken. This will not happen without a very clear business case describing and quantifying the benefits.

Since the constant transactions, from conversations to purchases, going on in digital systems and the massive data they generate can have such a dramatic effect on business performance and competitiveness, a failure to manage these digital systems effectively can have a very serious impact on the business as a whole. It should be a concern for top management in all companies that failing to align digital strategies to real business needs and to deliver optimal value to the business through all channels exposes the organization to risk and revenue loss.

Digital programs have been instrumental in growing the volume of touch points between organizations and their customers and suppliers. With this you should expect an increased focus on how digital systems can be used to add value to the business. But in most companies that I talk to data from different programs are analyzed independently of each other and much information, especially from the communications side of the business, the unstructured and mostly text-based data, is not properly studied at all. In many cases this has to do with lack of resources and shortage of digital talent sufficiently experienced in data analysis, but in too many companies this is ignored as inconsequential data. Data generated from customer behavior is never inconsequential—it is paramount for success. In the fast changing technology landscape and the turbulent economy we are in now the need to effectively manage digital resources and optimize performance has never been greater.

In data-driven organizations, however, it is increasingly recognized that all business units have a pivotal role to play in driving digital strategy and governance practices forward. In these companies critical business processes often span multiple business units and directors rely on information provided by digital systems for their decision-making. This calls for horizontal teamwork for developing, implementing, running and measuring the effect of digital programs. The new insight into business areas from this model provides many opportunities for innovation and new thinking as a diversity of talent come together, but it may also create some major headaches when people with strong digital knowledge are hired into units not accustomed to hire or manage such talent. Therefore, change management plays an important role in implementing digital strategy and governance into an organization for the first time and must be clearly addressed in the business case.

The current economic situation in most places of the world today has created a climate of cost reduction and budget restrictions. This has resulted in an era where resources involved in a corporation's digital ecosystem must be used as efficiently as possible while managing the escalating growth of digital platforms and customer touch-points. This reality demands that steps are taken to organize external resources ready for the next cycle of growth and new developments. This prompts the need for new and agile processes and strong supplier governance to avoid costly budget overruns and damaging customer service failures. Of course, I am not saying that using suppliers is bad. I am a hired resource myself, but the relationship works better for all parties if properly managed with clear goals and objectives. Again, supplier governance must be addressed in the business case.

Putting together a cross organizational team and developing a business case that provides a high level set of business arguments for digital strategy and governance is a must for a company looking to compete for customers now and in the future. A good business case should explain how a strategy process and governance initiative covering the entire digital ecosystem could enable a company and the executives that run it to:

- Realize the financial upside awaiting them through innovation, increased sales, customer loyalty and cost savings through process efficiencies, trained employees and improved systems, etc.

- Be aware of all related risks likely impacting their organization if things remain the same, if ad hoc fixes are implemented or if new systems are installed without a strategy and performance measurement tied to business goals.

- Understand the benefits in improving the management processes to manage these risks, find opportunities in the market and fuel innovation.

- To see cultural and business advantages of better managed relationships with suppliers, service providers and other stakeholders.

- Capitalize on the critical aspects of governance such as transparent and understandable communication of all activities and management processes to satisfy management and other interested stakeholders.

- Believe that a greater sense of security can lead to healthy risk taking that again can produce new market opportunities.

Although digital strategy and governance are focused on systems with an interface that use and generate data they also cover the culture, organization, policies and practices that provide oversight and transparency through the organization and optimize results through performance management. Ideally, the process should be part of wider corporate business strategy and governance activities but can also be run as a stand-alone process functioning as an amendment to the existing business strategy. Rarely though, if this process is done properly and thoroughly, will the business strategy remain as is without revisions after implementation of the digital strategy and performance measurement starts. Digital programs and the data they generate are now so intertwined in all aspects of a business that new discoveries in the form of innovation and improved processes are inevitable. Therefore, digital strategy cannot and should not be treated as an add-on.

To conclude: the business case for digital strategy and governance should clearly articulate the benefits of strategic value creation; good risk management, data analysis, oversight, and clear communication as it supports the organization's business goals, reduces the cost and prevents failures. A good business case engenders greater trust, teamwork and confidence in the people trusted with digital services who today are a growing talent base in most companies. And with today's digital talent war a best-in-class business case will show how a solid strategy and governance of digital systems and programs could help attract and retain the best people.

⑩ Preparedness for Today and Inevitable Change

One thing is for certain; things change. And with all things digital change is rapid and disruptive. New software solutions, communication platforms, and devices for access and sharing are developed and launched at an exponential rate. Many of these present new and unique opportunities brands can and should take advantage of, and many do, but more often than not these new solutions enter an organization organically, under the radar and without strategy or governance. A few years back when Facebook took off as a corporate marketing channel, a global company could within weeks have a dozen company pages in multiple languages without as much as a user guideline or a process for storing log-in passwords in place. Management's awareness of risks related to the company's digital ecosystem has increased, but mostly on the system level. Risk related to digital programs is therefore seen as an IT problem. It is not. Every business unit engaged in digital programs to capture business opportunities needs to have a process in place to minimize risks associated with them. Still today I talk with companies where they have or are contemplating entering new platforms without basic governance. This type of activity still flies under the radar or is ignored by many corporations because they do not feel the pain of not doing it right. That is until something happens.

In the wake of major accidents and corporate scandals where the public has gone online to vent their frustration and to have their say, companies finally see the need to have governance and processes in place to guard and monitor their brand online. But with this new management awareness often comes the question: what are we doing here? This question cannot be answered with clicks, likes and views. Management wants to know toward which business goals are our resources being spent and what are we getting in return. Of course it is not just fear that drives management's desire to have more control over their digital platforms. The plethora of articles about the benefits of big data or utilizing the data available to improve the way business is conducted and how customer and stakeholder engagement can increase loyalty and make it easier to do business has created a rush to cash in on these opportunities. For these and many other reasons digital strategy and governance has become a topic discussed at the very top of an organization.

Together, threat and opportunity have created a growing realization that more management commitment is needed to improve the results, accountability, management and control of digital activities. But there is a long way to go before that growing realization becomes real-world practice. In my experience, having been involved in hundreds of digital projects, I see a general lack of accountability and not enough shared ownership and clarity of responsibilities for digital services and projects. The communication between internal stakeholders and different providers of digital services both from within the organization itself and its external partners has to improve and be based on joint accountability for all initiatives. In many corporations there is a widening gap between what the different business units and their partners think the business requires and what the business thinks the business units are able to deliver. To narrow that gap organizations need to obtain a better understanding of the value delivered by the digital ecosystem today and the potential that lies within. It is essential for the business case that both internal and external suppliers articulate the measures that are required, in business terms, to achieve this end and that they are planning to measure performance moving forward in a way that is shared by all parties and report in a structure that can help move the company forward towards shared goals. A lack of clarity and transparency in reporting leads to uncertainties when making significant decisions which in turn can lead to reluctance to take the necessary risks resulting in failure to seize opportunities.

—— 0 ——

Stakeholders need to be clearly identified and addressed in the business plan—your argument for developing digital strategy and governance for the business—to allow for buy-in and proper mandates. One set of stakeholders will always be top management. In some cases you will address them first in a simplified business case to get the resources to develop the full business case addressing all stakeholders. For the simplified business case, top management, wants to understand how their organization is doing in digital in comparison with competitors and other relevant benchmark organizations. In addition they want estimates on costs and potential earnings and outlines of opportunities and risks. Because organizations are relying more and more on digital platforms and systems to supply data essential to decision making in addition to customer and stakeholder transactions and interaction, management needs to be aware of critical risks and whether they are being managed. To provide these answers the teams set to manage the digital ecosystem need to understand whether the infrastructure underpinning today's and tomorrow's programs and the digital systems and platforms they run on are capable of supporting expected business needs. Everyone involved understands that estimates in the simplified business case are rough approximations. Estimating the cost of revitalizing an ecommerce program needs immense data analysis and evaluation of available options. The simplified business case will outline the work needed and give a cost range and an increased earnings range. The real numbers will materialize in the full business case.

The full business case needs to show that digital systems, platforms and communications and the data they generate are complex and have their own rapidly changing and unique conditions. The need to apply sound management disciplines and controls are increasingly important for the safekeeping of the enterprise and this cannot be achieved without a thorough digital strategy and governance process. Once an organization decides to embark on that journey, based on the simplified case, it is vital that all internal and external stakeholders are clearly identified. These are not personas or users of the system, but the stakeholders directly involved in the decision-making process. Their input and buy-in for the process and outcome are crucial. The list of stakeholders will vary from company to company but the following are part of most processes.

As stated, top management sits on top of the list. They are looking ahead to future business goals, and are concerned about the safe keeping of their brand as an asset and making sure that their company is keeping pace with competition. Next on the list are the heads of all business units with profit and loss responsibilities where the digital ecosystem's performance increasingly has an impact on business results. Within the business units you have stakeholders with responsibilities for vital communication tasks such as investor, government and public relations. Another important stakeholder group is middle level business, marketing, communications and IT management. They will be tasked with running and managing the strategy under the new governance. A successful business case is dependent on their input and buy-in and that there is a process to help these managers with anchoring the business case and the changes it implies within their teams. And also on the list are the key external stakeholders including key business partners and suppliers, shareholders, and customers.

When developing a business case for digital strategy and governance it is important to try to address the concerns of these stakeholders in a direct a quantifiable manner.

Concerns they typically have when it comes to strategy and governance include:

- Performance measurement to make sure the digital ecosystem delivers at best-in-class levels.

- Data mining programs are initiated and reports delivered to fuel innovation based on customer input.

- Uptime and access to information and services on digital platforms for all stakeholders and the security and continuity of the platforms these services are running on.

- Costs of implementing changes to digital platforms and systems.

- Costs of running and maintaining digital programs, setting business-related KPIs and—where possible—identifying measurable returns on investments.

- The process of assuring quality and reliability of service that builds brands with reduced risk of embarrassments.

- Assurance that staff and vendors in charge of the digital ecosystem are responding to the real needs of the business dynamically and with real insight.

- Clear and actionable identification and management process of risks to the business from digital systems and platforms including mobilization and protocols during crisis scenarios.

- Honest identification of internal capabilities and skills and the process for ongoing training within all critical aspects of running and maintaining the digital ecosystem.

- Compliance with legal, regulatory and contractual requirements both in regards to internal compliance and ethics regulations and the laws of countries where the company conducts business.

- Description of the digital ecosystem's nimbleness in response to changing conditions and the processes in place to make sure that the systems are maintaining relevance to the business and its stakeholders.

- Integration of software that runs vital business services, collection of data including measurement, reporting and responsiveness to change.

- Flexibility to address special and ongoing needs from business units.

As these topics are addressed and detailed in the business case, investments will likely be needed to improve and develop them. Therefore, it is important to begin with as good a definition as possible of the potential benefits from such an initiative to help build a viable business case. The expected benefits can then become the project success criteria and subsequently be monitored for future reporting to validate the business case.

The benefits from a thorough digital strategy and governance project will often include:

- Better reporting and measurement practices collectively from the company's digital ecosystem

- Faster capture of opportunities and threats

- Ongoing optimization of programs

- Improved cooperation between business units

- Topline growth

- Improved protection of reputation and brand

- Increased customer satisfaction and loyalty

- Improved customer centric innovation

- Better transparency and accountability for internal and external stakeholders

- Improved transparency of costs and processes that run the digital ecosystem (platforms, systems) across business units and the suppliers/vendors they deploy

- Increased internal and external transparency, control and accountability of the data the systems generate and store

- Clarified decision-making accountabilities and definitions of internal and supplier user and provider relationships.

The business case should also make a point of showing a return on initial and ongoing investments from the proposed digital strategy that returns stakeholder value. This includes improved understanding of overall investment costs for all systems and programs along with estimated annual budgets for running, maintaining and updating them. You can show this through ROI cases explaining how the investments in the different elements, alone or in synergies, will benefit the company. In addition to showing the value of investments the business case must identify focused and prioritized cost cutting with clear reasons and benefits for the areas that need increased investments. It must detail how the project will avoid unnecessary expenditures, and that needed expenditures are demonstrably matched to business goals either directly or indirectly. To bolster your arguments for the needed investments in infrastructure or resources it is important to identify the risks that may imply for internal stakeholders if the investments are not made or if reduced investments in areas that may impact their business are suggested when leadership is evaluating the business case. Managers will also like to have clarified how the improved system will change or contribute to their key performance indicators. People care about their bonuses.

The digital strategy and governance project can enhance business partnerships. If this is a goal for your business you should make sure the business case details how the new processes and the performance measurement program will streamline partner communication, improve software integration of partner-shared systems, and utilize data from the whole system to measure and improve performance. If possible, show how the new strategy will provide routes to realize new partner opportunities, facilitate joint ventures with other companies, and identify areas that may not receive attention or sponsorship today. An integrated governance structure across business units will increase management and communication complexity, but if it is done right it can facilitate better relationships with key partners, vendors and suppliers that will increase efficiency and reduce total spend on external resources. Most likely business management, product development, customer service, human resources, marketing, sales and other teams will be using different vendors and suppliers for their enterprise resource planning (ERP), customer relationship management (CRM), employee and recruitment management, content management systems (CMS), and other software solutions. These are specialized solutions and vendor partners, but it will nevertheless benefit the company to identify how these platforms can work together and simplify management processes to reduce risk and cost.

There is an expectation that strengthening strategy and governance should result in performance improvement of the digital ecosystem across the board. To that end there must be a clear identification of whether a digital service or project supports existing business practices or is intended to provide future added value for the company in order to avoid unrealistic expectations. A focus on the performance improvement of the programs will lead to the attainment of best practices through an increased ability to benchmark performance through data collection and reporting. Increased reporting on agreed-upon performance measures will lead to increased transparency, which again should raise the bar for the performance of internal stakeholders, and the business case should promote the expectation that the bar should continuously be raised.

Other benefits to your company that your business case could outline are that digital strategy's participation in business strategy and vice versa will improve your company's responsiveness to market challenges and opportunities. An anchored digital governance can achieve a consistent approach to taking risks regarding the integration of emerging platforms and communication with external stakeholders, and a strong governance enables an integrated approach to meeting external legal and regulatory requirements regarding data collection, privacy, etc.

—— 0 ——

Finally, it is important to emphasize that an enterprise-wide team and communication approach must be adopted when implementing a digital strategy and its governance structure. A shared, cohesive view of the strategy and its governance is needed across the enterprise with a common reporting language and KPIs that are anchored in the company's business goals. Leaders of your business units and the owners of digital systems, services and platforms must work together to define and control requirements based on the processes outlined in the governance. There should be a clear understanding and approval by stakeholders of what is within the scope of digital governance and what sits within the corporate governance. Owners of the different digital programs will need to develop control models that satisfy the needs of all business units. Therefore, a control committee approach that ensures anchoring is recommended for the ongoing monitoring of your strategy's direction and performance. The committee members or the organization should not regard this as an additional management task. This is an opportunity to be on the front line when customer data are analyzed and discussed. Depending on the volume of data and the importance of the digital systems to the business, such a group could meet at any time from weekly to annually.

Your proposed governance plan—organizational structure and framework for defining processes and the controls required to manage them—needs to be addressed in the business case. This includes top-level commitment where they provide a mandate for the management teams and a direction backed up by clear accountability through performance measures and KPIs. These are necessities for the digital governance to succeed in practice and must be emphasized in the business case. In addition to the top-level mandate it is essential to make sure management responsibilities and accountabilities are outlined and defined so managers are clear about their roles. This is required for an executable business case although it may generate challenges and pushbacks since digital governance management structures will often work across corporate silos, so be prepared for possible turf wars if top management is not clear in their direction or do not fully participate in the process. It is important to ensure a good balance between the centrally driven policy and locally implemented practices and to avoid too much bureaucracy. Incentives should be considered to motivate adherence to the framework. Since the processes for digital governance often need to be integrated with other enterprise-wide governance practices, or parts of them such as vendor management and legal compliance and ethics, you should make sure your proposal is clearly informed by existing practices.

For your plan to work trust and buy-in for the strategy and governance needs to be attained from the owners of digital systems, services and platforms, whether they are in-house or external suppliers. The suppliers of services must be seen as professional, expert and aligned to customer needs and interest. Trust has to be developed by whatever means including awareness programs and joint workshops. You should outline this in your business case.

Every program has KPIs rooted in the business unit's short- and long-term goals. It is necessary to detail in the business case how these KPIs will be measured and how and when they will be presented along with steps that will be taken if the strategies fall short of goals. Proper measurement programs will ensure that objectives are owned and monitored. Depending on management practices, the creation of a balanced scorecard[1] for some organizations could underpin and reinforce achievement of digital objectives. Digital transactions are highly measurable through a wide variety of analytics tools and in my experience the creation of an initial set of measures based on current transactions creates a good base line that shows the programs' starting point. In some companies they will be looking at some of these numbers for the first time, such as social media and mobile transactions, providing some "a-ha moments" and that can be a very good way to raise awareness for your proposed digital governance program. "We can only go up from here", or "I did not know that this is actually going on" are statements you will hear, but remember, the measures used must be in business terms and be approved by stakeholders. "Likes" and "engagement" can only be used if the business case can define their meaning in business terms and quantify its benefit to the business.

As an overall reminder for your work on a digital strategy and governance business case is always to keep a strong focus on costs and increase in earnings and always to keep it anchored in the goals the strategy is set to achieve. This should always be presented quantitatively. It is likely that there will be opportunities to make financial savings as a consequence of implementing improved digital strategies and governance,

---

1   The balanced scorecard (BSC) is a strategy performance management tool—a semi-standard structured report, supported by design methods and automation tools, that can be used by managers to keep track of the execution of activities by the staff within their control and to monitor the consequences arising from these actions. It is perhaps the best known of several such frameworks (it was the most widely adopted performance management framework reported in the 2010 annual survey of management tools undertaken by Bain & Company). Since its original incarnation in the early 1990s as a performance measurement tool, the BSC has evolved to become an effective strategy execution framework. The BSC concept as put forth by Drs Robert S. Kaplan and David P. Norton is now seen as a critical foundation in a holistic strategy execution process that, besides helping organizations articulate strategy in actionable terms, provides a road map for strategy execution, for mobilizing and aligning executives and employees, and making strategy a continual process. Source: Wikipedia.

but it is just as important to also detail a possible increase in earnings.. Earnings properly outlined and defined will help to gain support for the business case.

Present your business case along with an effective communication and awareness campaign. If your proposal gets the green light it needs to be clearly communicated to all stakeholders and the company as a whole so that objectives are understood and practices are complied with.

PART III
The Brand

(11) Symbiotic Relationship between Brand and Digital Strategy

At the foundation of digital strategy, as for all customer-facing strategies, lies the brand and the sentiments it provokes along with the organization's understanding and buy-in of its mission, vision and values. An understanding of this symbiotic relationship between brand and digital strategy is a key success factor because clarity of message, tone and self are essential for relevant engagement throughout your digital ecosystem. Well-crafted positioning and segmented and persona-based value propositions allow you to capture the attention of your target audience's non-linear search for information. A digital strategy can become pure mechanics without a well-articulated brand to back it up. So, when I sit down with a company to discuss digital strategy we start with the state of the brand.

Brands organically change over time. This is not necessarily a negative, but for many organizations this organic process can bring the different elements of a brand out of alignment and this can distort your image and your positioning both internally and externally—and that is a negative.

Distortions and misrepresentations of the visual language of your brand are the easiest to identify—where templates, colors, fonts, image use and other tangibles have deviated from the guidelines, thereby posing an unaligned and sometimes confusing image to stakeholders or in worst case result in situations where the brand's visual language becomes less defensible to plagiarism and other abuse. More difficult to spot is when your brand has become unclear in the minds of your customers due to inconsistency or lack of clear positioning, and this brand dissonance starts to produce a negative effect on your business performance. This is when your brand "self," how your company identifies itself and thusly how it's perceived by stakeholders, is out of alignment. This can, if not corrected, have severe consequences for an organization over time. How do you onboard new talent or introduce a new product or service if there is a difference in perception of the brand from those on the inside and outside of the company? This scenario can have a drastic impact on hiring, sales and customer loyalty and must be addressed and fixed. At some point Microsoft went from hot and innovative to corporate and stagnant, but the realization of this happened at different times for those on the inside and those on the outside of the company. This resulted in products such as the Zune,[1] which I do not think anybody quite understood.

---

1 The Zune media player, hardware version, was introduced in November 2006 five years after Apple released the first iPod and only eight months before Apple introduced the iPhone. Microsoft officially discontinued the device in October 2011 after having failed to capture significant market share.

Defining and developing a strong brand and holding the organization in balance by keeping the brand aligned is not optional. To do this you must follow carefully crafted steps, checks and balances in a well-defined process because branding is a science as much as an art form.

The term "brand" properly refers to the sentiments and connotations your visual language and positioning evoke for all your stakeholders. For stakeholders your brand embodies your company's mission, vision, and values—not as they are written down, but as they are realized. It is your stakeholders' actions that will determine the success of your company's products and services. The brand's existence hangs in the balance. Each touch point will either erode or strengthen your brand.

All brands have two components:

- Brand Elements—the name, logo, logotype, shapes, colors, products, and services by which a company is represented and ultimately recognized. These elements can be touched, seen, and easily defined.

- Brand Self—the more intangible, but equally vital, brand component. It resides in sentiments, feelings and beliefs, at the crossroads of your elevator pitch and the mission, vision, and values of your company.

It is the second component, the brand self, that most often comes into question when an organization finds itself at a crossroad contemplating major decisions for its future during the development of a digital strategy. For the success of a digital strategy and governance process it is vital that your brand is in alignment and your organization collectively supports your mission, vision and values.

To get started you must craft positioning statements for your company and its products and services. These statements will serve as the foundation for further messaging work with the goal of shaping your audience's perception of your brand. For an audience to receive your message they must have an understanding of why they should listen to you in the first place. This understanding will vary product-to-product and audience-to-audience. Therefore companies must craft segmented and persona-based value propositions for their products and services.

Persona-based value propositions are even more critical in this hyper-connected world of content overload where consumers demand that brands engage with them—build and maintain connections with them. According to a new study from Edelman,[2] brands are failing to perform in just that. The researchers surveyed 11,000 online consumers, in eight countries, who participated in a minimum of one brand-engaging activity in the previous year. The study found that 90 percent of these consumers want marketers to more effectively share their brands. Yet on average, only 10 percent think any given brand does this well. Online conversations through social media are the first step toward brands sharing with people of all ages. On an average, 40 percent of consumers want brands to engage in more meaningful conversations with them. This presents an interesting dilemma since most brands and companies are not created to or do not have the culture to have interesting and meaningful discussions about their products. For many brands this will

---

2 Fall of 2013.

put transparency and honesty on trial even if the biggest gap between importance and performance in the Edelman study was in the area of "communicating openly and transparently about how products are sourced and made." Brand dissonance with consumers exemplified here accentuates the symbiotic relationship between your brand and your digital strategy. While 54 percent of respondents considered social media conversations an important area for brands to build and maintain connections with them, just 12 percent believed that the statement applied to their favorite brands, leading me to believe that brands we love are cut some slack, and maybe that is why they fall so hard when they fall. A sound digital strategy can help reduce that risk.

Bottom line is that consumers feel that brands underperform in asking them about their needs, with 51 percent seeing this as important and only 10 percent feeling that brands are doing this well, revealing a 41 percent point gap from desired action to actual action. Consumers also want complete openness about product performance with nine out of 10 wanting to know how products are made and how they should perform against competitors. In addition, 47 percent of the respondents want brands to be more transparent about how products are sourced and manufactured, 43 percent want brands to do more to give something back to the communities in which they operate.

In a consumer-oriented digital strategy dealing with and improving sharing, dialog, transparency and customer input should be your focus areas. And to accomplish this, your brand must be clearly defined in the language of your audience so they can place or position you in the space in which you operate and it must be further refined through well-crafted persona-based value propositions. If there is a sense that your brand might not be correctly positioned for optimized future growth in the digital space you should consider a brand re-alignment process in tandem with your digital strategy work. I recommend running the processes together where fact-finding overlaps, so your organization does not tire from repeated inquiries and too much time is taken away from valuable resources. The brand process is a series of exercises constructed to identify where the current brand sentiments may not fit with future business strategies, digital strategies and goals and how the company looks today. This will not only help shape or realign the brand but also inform your digital strategies and set performance measures for your brand moving forward.

(12) Developing Brand Positioning and Value Propositions

You can take several approaches to brand development work, but most brands will go through a process similar to what is outlined here. Sometimes branding firms give their own names to the different phases and deliveries in a brand process to make them seem proprietary, but it boils down to fact finding, self-realization and a creative and strategic output of these two combined.

During a brand or brand re-alignment process there is not always a need for formal, primary research, but steps must be taken to properly gauge the status of the brand in the minds of all major internal and external stakeholder groups.[1] For internal stakeholders the process must ensure ownership of

---

1 External stakeholders in this context are a broad group containing among others, customers, business partners, investors, etc.

the process and the result, and for all stakeholders the final output must be something they can buy into and believe in.

The discovery phase is much like the procedure of a good investigative journalist, people are interviewed and all available information is gathered to get to the bottom of the things that your company's varied audience members care about in order to identify the true brand story. The goal here is to uncover the truth about who you are as a company, why this is relevant and why target audiences should care.

I will not go into too much detail about this initial phase as for the most part it mirrors the insights and analysis part of the digital strategy process outlined in the next section, but below are some key areas you should touch upon:

- In-depth interviews with executives, managers of programs and key employees who are in direct contact with customers

- In-depth interviews with customers and partners

- Review of industry and secondary research

- Review of company data and plans

- Analysis of the qualitative data available in your industry's digital ecosystem to show how existing and prospective customers make choices in the marketplace, and how customers perceive the brand at each touch point

- Big data: Pull down text data from the internet and analyze what your target audience is saying about your brand and the industry you are in

- Conducting a benchmarking study of competitors' and their brand messaging

- Developing a brand-focused S.W.O.T. (Strengths, Weaknesses, Opportunities, and Threats) analysis

- Building personas based on optimal, prioritized customers (character sketches based on the data collected).

It must be kept in mind that the point of this research phase is to satisfy stakeholders, most importantly customers, by finding the brand story that matters to them. However, no brand should be everything to everyone. Selecting and ranking the audiences to which you wish to communicate and "sell" is a key success factor along with selecting and ranking the actions you want taken by your selected audience(s) at the different brand touch points—stores, website, social media, etc.

To stay stakeholder focused during the branding process create personas as reference points for your development. To create the personas that truly represent your varied stakeholders use all your research and analysis to identify your key audiences and their needs. From this data you can build the personas, or "character sketches," for each audience group. I prefer fairly substantial and rich personas and give them names and identify and specify their individual needs, backgrounds, and reasons to conduct business with your company. You can use the same personas developed for the digital strategy process, but the description of their goals and sentiments and other

emotional values may differ in order to better match the issues your brand is facing. These role-play models provide a real context for discussing the needs of customer types and for testing your ideas.

Personas are character sketches representing not only stakeholders but also common goals and concerns we should address.

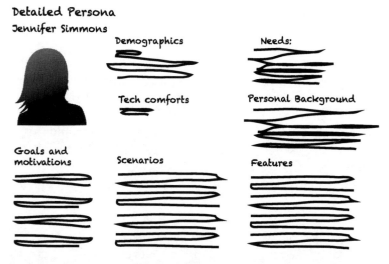

Figure 12.1   A typical persona or character sketch

Armed with the analysis you have created based on your research and the character sketches that personify the facts and insight, the core team spearheading the brand-positioning project can go to work.

Positioning is the technique by which companies try to define an image or identity for a product, service, brand, or company in the minds of stakeholders in their target markets. Positioning takes place in the mind of the prospect and not on the paper it is written on. By that I mean that positioning is an active process and the ultimate engagement. You tell your stakeholder who you are and they process it and tell it back to you. That is your positioning. So by active I mean that it is floating and will always change by what surrounds you, your industry and your stakeholders. If you are currently in food related industry you might say that floating is too mild of a term to use. With the popularity of the Atkinson's Diet a few years back the perception of carbohydrates changed for a large part of the population. If you were a pasta manufacturer you went from good to bad in the minds of many consumers almost overnight. Other industries are thankfully much more stable. Bicycling is by most seen as a positive. So a bike related brand process will focus on quality of product, the behaviors of your company, styling, price point, use, etc. "Hey, wait a minute", you might say. "What if they use athletes to endorse their product and they get caught..." Yeah, that's another story.

In the process of developing your brand strategy it is important to analyze how potential stakeholders perceive your company compared to their perceptions of your competitors in the context of the state of your industry. When you work on your positioning leave the inspirational to the development of slogans and taglines and focus on reality, true differentiation, and who you are.

—— 0 ——

Clearly the way to build brand identity today is different from what it was in the recent past. One look at the overwhelming visual noise in today's market makes it even more challenging to establish a truly new and unique brand. Challenging, yes, but entrepreneurs and digital disruptors make it happen. Some brands just emerge because they are truly unique and there is a clear desire in the market for that specific type of product, such as Tesla. Others emerge from familiar territories but are better or sometimes it is just market timing. Spotify is an example of perfect market timing. Even if your brand hits the right note with your audience remember that no level of governance structure will keep your brand aligned over time if it is not clearly defined towards all audiences on all interaction platforms. This is a process you must do regardless. As a solid start your brand should be evaluated and differentiated through the creation of:

- Identity—a definition of your company

- Brand self—mission, vision, and values

- Strategic targets—a definition of your customers[2]

- Brand positioning statements—how you reflect or desire to reflect in your customers' minds

- Elevator pitch—how you sell the essence of your company

- Brand space—a description of where you communicate

- Brand character—the connotations that describe your brand

---

2 We use the term customer here to signify all stakeholders.

- Brand language—design, voice, image use, and style

- Messages and themes—specific communications

- Reasons to believe—articulated benefits of working with your company.

When that is done all brand "actions" must be aligned and refer to the definitions above. Do not expect that your employees in your sales office in Malaysia will intuitively understand the brand you created ten years ago on a different continent. You need to have guidelines and processes that allow your teams to "translate" and understand your brand across cultures. This creates strong companies and brands where employees can focus and customers create relationships based on trust— loyalty.

For the development of digital strategies persona-based value propositions is probably your most important tool. While your "vision" steers your company in the right direction, "mission" specifies why we are heading in that direction and "values" in what fashion we should get there—value propositions are the tangible statements that connect a company with its stakeholders. If your value propositions are created correctly they can drive business for your company and traffic to your content.

To craft powerful value propositions we must systematize the information from our facts and insights phase:

- Who your company is (the products and services/values and goals)

- What your company offers that others don't or can't

- Which industries are targeted; what motivates them and what are their needs

- Who are the personas within those industries for your company's products and services

- What are your customers', potential customers', and web visitors' actual unmet wants and needs (real feedback from personas is required here)

- What tangible benefits/business results can your proposition claim that align precisely with the types of things your personas really want and need

- What do your competitors claim as their value propositions for the same personas

- How do your value propositions differentiate you from your competitors

- How can the value proposition you arrived at be creatively shaped through a content marketing strategy to be optimally persuasive and drive action that is beneficial for your audience and your company.

Inherent in the vast data that we have collected and analyzed are things we must know to create sound value propositions aided by the creative and strategic input by the team involved.

In Figure 12.2, you can see that it is not enough for a company to have industry knowledge and input from customers as the building blocks for the company to extract a differentiating value proposition. To create value propositions that work—

that will drive desired target behaviors—you must employ informed, creative strategies that add direction to the value proposition.

Multiple data sets leading to clear insights imbuing a sound strategy is a must, but creativity is the deciding factor between a truly differentiating, strong value proposition and a weak one.

In other words, without sufficient strategy and creativity behind the value proposition creation, the proposition is unlikely to drive the business in the direction you want it to take.

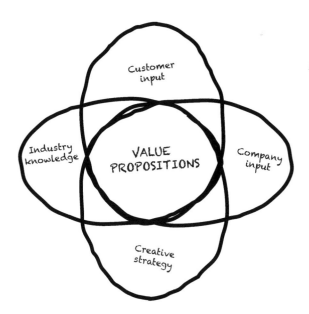

Figure 12.2   Value proposition model

SEGMENTATION OF INDUSTRIES AND THEIR PERSONAS

In the Figure 12.3, each stakeholder segment served by the company is viewed as a unique target that is imbued with its own special wants/needs, and consequently, its own special value propositions that will offer demonstrable solutions for these needs. Additionally, within each stakeholder segment, there are proof points that will resonate specifically with each of the personas within the identified segment. You might ask yourself is this is truly necessary. This is a lot of work! Yes it is, but consider the few seconds your paid search ad has to resonate with your audience and generate a click. Then, take a look at the average bounce rate on your campaign landing pages. Clear and targeted value propositions will help you improve both metrics and increase conversion. What would that be worth for your company? Better leads and increased sales—working on your value propositions are worth it!

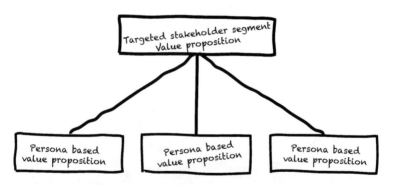

Figure 12.3   Targeted stakeholder segment

1.0   Targeted Stakeholder Segment Value Proposition: This statement touches on all the value proof points the company has towards a stakeholder segment they target to serve.

2.0   Persona Based Value Proposition: These statements focus the value proof points toward the benefits for specific audiences within target segments.

(13) UX-based Brand Workshop Model

Developing strong, segmented value propositions will enable a better ROI on the tactical elements of your digital strategy such as campaigns and website conversion paths, but as discussed earlier it is greatly beneficial to have a well-defined brand to guide your teams to create a holistic statement out of the plethora of platforms and programs they will be creating or changing to drive your strategies. For the purposes of digital strategy development I prefer to do this brand definition work in a digital context.

In workshop settings where the goal is to get a core group of stakeholders to kick off a brand definition and alignment process, a user experience (UX)-based brand-building model, I developed while working with a large retail chain, is a good tool. It helps the group visualize the brand in the minds of stakeholders by picturing a familiar setting. For companies and the people that shape them it is most often best to use tangible or familiar models or visuals when developing the more abstract *brand self* defined as your mission, vision and values.

We build personas to help guide us through the process of discussing what our stakeholders want or need to avoid constant references back to the vast amounts of data and information collected during the facts and insights phase. Similarly, we want a visual framework for the development of mission, vision, values, positioning, and our persona-based value propositions. This visual framework should allow us to talk to all stakeholders and address all sides of the company. I have seen people use "magazines" and all kinds of sticky note processes to create visual frameworks for brand development, but a magazine falls short in scope and the brown paper with the sticky notes tends to lose half the room.

The corporate website, however, is the arena where companies address all stakeholders and provide information about what they do and whom they serve.

- Here we tell the world who we are and why we exist

- Here we position our products and services

- Here we address customers, partners, employees, politicians, NGOs, investors, media, etc.

- Here we build sentiments and connotations through visuals, animations, words, videos, etc.

In a workshop format we are able to use this multi-level website model along with company-specific personas and draft a stakeholder-focused first draft of the components that make up the brand.

Figure 13.1   UX brand model

Front and center in the slider on top show how you would define what you do and why a potential new customer should stay around and not continue browsing. This visual framework has proved a great way to initiate a valuable exchange of opinions and ideas because everyone in the room clearly understands the task—it has a sense of reality to them. Yes, the web is going mobile and design esthetics change, but this large-screen, traditional web design model works for now. Using this framework you can express your *mission, vision,* and *values* through a video on the home page or described in the "about us" section depending on the type of company your are. Under "industries" we define our customers and the space in which we operate.

Brand positioning statements—how you reflect in customers' minds—live in the "solutions" page and the elevator pitch—

how you sell the essence of your company and its products—could get the lead in one of the homepage sliders.

Messages and themes—specific communications—can take shape in the "newsroom" or in the "investors" section. In "careers" you can describe your *reasons to believe*—articulated benefits of working with your company. Play around with the model and adapt the sections to match you company's profile.

One way to conduct this workshop is to project the empty website surrounded by personas on a whiteboard, or use a "Smartboard" if you have one, and then write down what the brand or website must communicate to meet the personas' needs and goals. The outcome could be in any format such as text, graphics, image, audio, video, or a combination of these formats. The key is to be creative and solve the messaging scenario. This allows people not commonly involved in these types of brand processes to let down their performance guard and participate fully in the process. They are present because we need their input.

When you use this framework as part of your digital strategy process it is always interesting to take the results from your workshop and compare it with your existing corporate website. I say "corporate" website because many companies such as Nike will have its nike.com that is consumer facing and nikeinc.com that addresses all stakeholders. Doing this comparison between live site and workshop model you might find you want to make some content changes right away through your CMS. Your call. You do not have to wait until the whole strategy process is done to make your changes. It is a website with a CMS. You can always change it again. Constant improvement is a good way for your teams to get accustomed to working.

(14) Implementation Strategy

An implementation strategy is essential to ensure that the new or re-aligned brand is truly adopted and integrated within the organization and clearly presented to external stakeholders. I recommend conducting the implementation in tandem with the introduction of your digital strategy so your employees and partners don't get overloaded with new introductions. Vital for such an implementation strategy is to identify, build and plan activities that will inform and create understanding, acceptance, ownership, and enthusiasm. Commonly, brand implementation will be a roll-out conducted in stages to ensure optimal timing for the buy-in of the re-aligned brand from both internal and external stakeholders. Participation and sense of ownership are essential ingredients when conducting internal activities such as workshops and digital education programs.

Introducing the re-aligned brand to external stakeholders is a completely different game. Changes to your brand are not necessarily a cause for celebration for your customers and other stakeholders such as investors. Brand implementation is often costly and if you loved the brand the way it was you don't want it to change. We were hired by a large financial institution to help with the public and digital part of their new visual language and re-aligned brand implementation. An important factor was to reduce risk from a possible consumer backlash on social media. The risk factor was high since the launch came on the heels of the recent financial crisis where financial institutions had already gotten a lot of heat for their handling of funds, and rolling out a new visual language and new brand is not exactly cheap. We did not want a heated online discussion on frivolous spending and waste if we could avoid it.

The re-branding had been necessary due to a series of mergers and acquisitions over the past decade leaving the brand fragmented from the outside looking in, but maybe most importantly for the thousands of employees from the inside looking out. Our job, however, was to deal with the public. Explaining the root cause for the re-brand was too complicated. Not that people would not understand it—never underestimate your audience—but they live busy lives and could really not care less about a long explanation of the pains and ailments of a large financial institution gobbling up other companies to meet their constant growth goals. Still, we wanted a valuable information exchange with the public in social media rather than try to gloss it over. Here is what happened:

The date selected for unveiling the new brand was November 11, 2011–11.11.11. Only two weeks before the big change we got an email from their e-business director. They had decided against the social media campaign ideas presented to them by their advertising agency and were looking for creative and engaging solutions. We quickly gathered a team for a brainstorming and that afternoon we presented our idea and a strategy.

Our idea was simple, on paper, but a real challenge to complete in a 12-day turn-around. The concept was a Facebook contest that would start at 11 o'clock on 11.11.11. From that point on the financial institution would give away NOK[1] 1,111 ($200) every 11th minute for 11 hours. The contest rules where simple: every eleventh minute we would post a question and a hint on how it would be rated.

How can we improve mobile banking?

Hint: We rate on humor. Funniest answer wins.

Every eleventh minute a winner was selected and posted on the brand's Facebook wall. Transparency was a key factor here, so to make that point to the public we decided to project the Facebook page on a large and prominent building in Oslo[2] to send the message—we are transparent and open. Use your mobile phone and post whatever you want, for the world to see, on our Facebook page.

To ignite the campaign we created a social media burst campaign 24 hours before campaign start. As it proved, viral spread by users would do the rest. Our client believed in the idea and hoped for 2,000 comments.

Eleven o'clock on Friday 11.11.11 rolled around. We were all logged on ... and then it started ... The comments came pouring in. It never stopped. The comments and advice were fantastic. Every eleven minutes a new happy winner. To put it in perspective:

---

1   NOK is the currency abbreviation for Norwegian Kroner.
2   The largest city and capital of Norway.

 ALWAYS ON

11 hours x 60 minutes x 60 seconds = 39.600 Seconds

In 11 hours we got 35,417 comments. In addition, the campaign saw a 30 percent increase in page likes in one day. The clients sitting in our campaign HQ could not believe their eyes and could not stop smiling.

This was a successful re-launch of a brand, but the risks are there anytime you change something that people care about or have an opinion about—and the risks have increased with social media. Just imagine what would have happened if today's media landscape had existed at the time of the New Coke launch.

> *On April 23, 1985, Coca-Cola, amid much publicity, attempted to change the formula of the drink with "New Coke". Follow-up taste tests revealed most consumers preferred the taste of New Coke to both Coke and Pepsi, but Coca-Cola management was unprepared for the public's nostalgia for the old drink, leading to a backlash. The company gave in to protests and returned to a variation of the old formula using high fructose corn syrup instead of cane sugar as the main sweetener, under the name Coca-Cola Classic, on July 10, 1985. Source: Wikipedia*

The public forced this top-five global brand to retract within seven weeks of launch in a world of printed papers, wired phones and television sets and mail delivered by carrier. Imagine what would have happened today? Just the thought of the impact from funny and creative "YouTubers" alone is enough to make you cringe on behalf of the brand. Then you pile on top of that the storm of posts on Twitter and Facebook and the bashing from teenagers on Snapchat and Instagram.

It would be devastating. Be careful how you communicate changes to your brand and make sure you have control over you digital ecosystem you can properly monitor and respond if a storm—positive or negative—should happen.

Brand is an ongoing process and a successful brand strategy is adaptive to changes in the business environment and to changing cultural factors. Every day boomers leave the workplace and millennials enter. To that end you should have in place an evaluation process with guided checkpoints to check if the brand is properly responding to the complex cultural changes underway and to new technologies that can change the anatomy of your business' ecosystem and thus vastly change the way your brand interacts with its stakeholders.

In all brand processes continuous adjustment is necessary, whether it is the way your educational program is set up, the way your partner programs are built or how your employees interact with your customers.

Whether you cater to people in the Business-to-Consumer (B2C) or the Business-to-Business (B2B) market segments, your customer relationships begin at the first encounter with your brand—be that a store visit, an online action such as an ecommerce purchase or a post on a friend's social media profile, news stories, press releases, or other online communications that present your brand to stakeholders.

The benefits of a strong and, properly formulated brand—positioning and value propositions—cannot be overstated. Your value propositions that create the foundation that underlie the strategic and creative creation of all communication, are many, including:

- Higher employee yield and retention

- Greater customer retention

- Increased market share in targeted market segments

- Brand advocates that initiate knowledge exchanges in social media unsolicited on your behalf

- Greater revenues.

These benefits for the company are logical, since they grew out of a brand re-alignment process that looked hardest at what matters most in selling; not what your company needs to accomplish, but what your customers and potential customers, employees and other stakeholders need. That is the heart and soul of a strong and aligned brand.

PART IV

The Strategy

⑮ Defining Digital Strategy and its Development Process

The customer no longer follows a linear path to purchase, nor are they tied to any single channel. They are using digital tools like never before, amplifying brand experiences without any relationship boundaries and demanding more service options as part of the product purchase. So the role of CMO needs to have that broader perspective of the customer experience journey and be prepared to generate appropriate content for that diversity.

Raj Rao, VP of Global eTransformation, 3M

Developing a digital strategy that drives companies toward business goals has become a business essential for progressive organizations. The realization is that a corporation cannot navigate properly without a plan and response mechanism for

133

all the transactions[1] that take place every second in the digital realm. Nor can an organization grasp the advantages that are inherent in analyzing the generated data correctly and shape products, services and communication to meet and exceed their stakeholder's demands. Surprisingly, however, very few companies today have holistic cross business unit digital strategies with cohesive performance measures and a unified reporting structure. This landscape is changing, but slower than the development of technology itself. That should be a frightening prospect for many.

For most companies there is also a definition problem. The question is: what is digital strategy? There are consultants from advertising to IT and everything in-between that will want to sell you their definition of the term. For me, digital strategy is about analyzing and optimizing the correlation of online and off-line customer behavior and the effect it has on total sales, customer loyalty, product segment growth, and innovation. In addition, a holistic digital strategy will look at the internal communication channels and processes needed to achieve the set goals.

Digital strategy will always be a subset of the business strategy and must therefore strive to achieve the same business goals and have a governance and performance measurement program that works in tandem with existing programs and processes. In this context the use of the term "digital strategy" is defined within the disciplines of strategic management, marketing strategy and business strategy, and as such digital strategy is the process of specifying an organization's vision, goals, opportunities and initiatives in order to identify and maximize the business benefits of digital programs, initiatives

---

1 Transaction in this context means all exchanges of money, information, images, video and text.

and platforms for the organization. IT or engineering-owned issues such as hardware and wired and wireless systems will not be addressed in this context unless they affect functions and accessibility such as download speeds, remote access to data or others that matter directly to users of the systems. In such cases the issue and the business case for needed change will be defined, but not the final solution or its implementation. Also, the digital strategy, in this business and customer centric context, does not set out to define the processes of developing new software systems. It may, however, refer to certain processes adapted by an organization such as agile development or scrum to illustrate how the strategies fit within existing frameworks.

In many corporations IT centric digital strategy, business centric digital strategy and online strategy tend to be discussed somewhat interchangeably. The differences between IT and business driven processes I outline above, however, there are also clear differences between digital and online strategies. Digital strategy takes a holistic view of all interactions with a company's content and data and the systems and functions that store them. Digital in this context connotes big data, deeper interactions with customers, more customized and personalized offerings and interactions, data driven decision making, and organizational models and processes that are more nimble and reactive to changes in the company's environment.

Online strategy, however, is focused on content and data accessed through a browser, including custom browsers such as mobile and web applications. Therefore, online is just a subset of digital, as there may be digital assets that are not online. In this context, a company may use the term "online strategy" limited to the development of plans to deploy their online assets to maximize business results and "digital strategy" as the more transformative step of changing the organization.

As with all business strategy work you do not have to attack the whole ecosystem at once. Organizations can deploy projects to improve specific areas or programs. I encounter these subsets of digital strategy quite often due to emerging platforms or because the strategic importance of improving certain programs can have for the company. These programs can include social media, ecommerce, recruitment, and knowledge management to name some. This divide and conquer approach can work if the company has a sound digital strategy and governance in place. If not you will most likely get into trouble somewhere along the line.

In other words, digital strategy can have an enterprise focus, which considers the broader opportunities and risks that digital potentially create. This includes customer intelligence, collaboration, new product/market exploration, sales and service optimization, enterprise technology architectures and processes, innovation and governance. But digital strategy can also have a more marketing and customer-focus such as web sites, mobile, ecommerce, social, site and search engine optimization, and advertising.

However, the term digital strategy should be reserved for a plan that takes the whole company's needs into consideration. Strategies that consider specific platforms and programs should be identified as such. This may seem semantic, but often it is the meaning we place on words that guides our view and actions. A sample hierarchy would be: your ecommerce strategy should adhere to the goals and governance set forth in the digital strategy just as the digital strategy should adhere to the goals and governance of the company's business strategy.

Figure 15.1   Strategy hierarchy

There are different approaches to developing a digital strategy, but at their core they all go through two phases:

1. In phase one research, facts and insights are gathered and analyzed for identifying the opportunities and/or challenges in your business where digital systems can provide a solution. This includes identifying the unmet needs and goals of your customers and other stakeholders that most closely align with those key business opportunities and/or challenges you are facing.

2. In phase two the analysis is developed into actionable strategies—from a vision of how your digital assets will fulfill business and customer needs, goals, opportunities

and challenges to a framework of connected programs with clear performance measures. The actionable strategies informed by the vision are developed and ordered based on priority and budget. Then implementation plans are developed for the prioritized digital initiatives so they can deliver on your vision.

There are a number of methodologies and processes that may be used to deliver on phase one and two. This chapter outlines a common set of steps that will lead to an executable holistic digital strategy that can fulfill on your vision. One of my goals it to abstain from using proprietary terms and use a set of common terms that should have similar meanings and definitions to most people.

⑯ Research, Facts and Insights

While researching reams of qualitative and quantitative data you are looking for opportunities and better solutions to market a product or service. You seek to find your audience and learn their behavior to better communicate your story to the world, build active and valuable information exchanges that the marketing industry now calls "engagement", build customer loyalty, that I think is better described as purchase preference, and sometimes most importantly—to build your brand. The key here is learning about your customers' behavior online and discovering patterns in seemingly random traffic and transactions. The fact that your brand exists online and possibly has a stellar digital ecosystem will not change people's behavior. You need to play to their ever-changing online habits.

This is a large and complex task, but it needs an agile and adaptive process. Developing a strategy is not a linear process—if you want to find the best ideas. Yes, it starts with research and goes through a series of common steps until implementation, but ideas can come at any point in the process. "Disruptive" ideas can make you review your data in a different light, start a new line of questioning during interviews, and make you go back and look over your findings again. Sometimes, however, the best solution is to stop—run a pilot to test your new findings or theses—analyze your results and look for ways to optimize. If your pilot was successful—can it scale? Test again and move forward with your strategy process. There are several benefits with this methodology:

- You will be working with real data quicker

- The team and the organization will see real-life progress and that motivates and inspires.

Keep the pilots short and concise. With the fast pace of digital you want your strategy process to be quick, dynamic and agile.

Following a strategy process, informed and injected with creative ideas, allows you to find innovative opportunities and solutions to complex problems. Therefore, it is vital to keep an open mind during all stages of your project and to allow room for the needed creativity. The strategy process should therefore be less rigid than the governance process that follows. So when you read the tasks outlined in this chapter remember it is not a step-by-step process but a description of the areas and methods you can use to uncover the information needed to develop a holistic digital strategy.

When you put together the team to develop the strategy make sure you have the needed experience for all areas you must cover. At least one member must have a solid digital background and a good understanding of platforms, systems, processes involved, people needed, traffic patterns, online behavior, user trends, etc. In addition the team must have solid knowledge of the industry the strategy will be implemented in or at the very least the team must have studied the industry up to a level where they can properly soak in the facts and insights and place them in relevant contexts. In Chapter 19, *Setting objectives: stakeholders and their requirements*, I will go further in depth on selecting your teams and defining your stakeholders. So for now let's say: with your team in place divide the tasks, set a deadline and start.

INTERVIEWS

A good place to start when learning about a company and its markets is to talk with, or rather listen to people. Obvious? Yes, but do companies do it? Surprisingly many don't. When you listen to people you do not get answers, but "feet-on-the-street" insight. People have their ideas of why things are and what they should be. When you pair what people say with data—then you see interesting things. New opportunities, progress hampering myths, inefficiencies, disconnected communication, waste and undiscovered innovation may be some of these.

Another important thing that happens when you listen to people is that you start the anchoring process. A strategy has a better chance of successful implementation if anchored properly within the company. Listening is a better anchoring device than informing and asking for buy-in. So when you are selecting internal stakeholders for interviews keep the anchoring process in mind.

I like to keep an open interview style where I follow an interviewee rather than lead him or her with a list of pre-set questions. This requires that the person conducting the interviews has experience with the industry and an understanding of the role the interview subject performs. The interviews should be recorded, transcribed and then boiled down to essentials.

Figure 16.1   Dialog

Interviews can be conducted as one-on-one discussions, group sessions or workshops. The interview list will often start with the company's senior management to get a clear idea of business goals from their own mind and not the PowerPoint crafted by the communications department. I like to follow that with a frank conversation on what they want to achieve by this strategy process. That is important, because in the end they will have to be the force behind implementation and performance management. They will essentially own the strategy. Next on the list is management that will own sections of the strategy—the management teams from marketing and sales, IT, operations and service stakeholders such as customer service and human resources with a goal of understanding their business goals, challenges and opportunities, products, organization, processes, supply chain, vendors, distributors, customers, and competitive landscape, as well as the potential role of their existing online assets.

But don't let the list stop with management and leaders of the different business units and service teams. Digital systems often have an interface. Talk to the people that work with these interfaces. They work in the warehouse, with data entry, customer service, human resources, accounting, they could be editors, content creators, social media managers, etc. They will present daily challenges that could uncover new processes needed, resource shortfalls, lack of training, and reasons why chunks of data are missing or why they are present. If a system is not performing optimally, habits and organic processes tend to be created to compensate. This is valuable information for any company and vital for creating a successful strategy.

Customers are the most important stakeholders for any company, but the problem or the beauty is that there are so many of them, and in most cases they are a very varied bunch of individuals from different geographic and demographic backgrounds. Surveys, can reach a much wider audience than physical meetings can ever do and can therefore provide valuable quantitative input to uncover the existing customer experience and their unmet needs and wants. But nothing beats listening to people face-to-face or over the phone to create a valuable exchange of information. So even if talking to a brand's customers in focus groups or one-on-one can never have the reach of a well-conducted survey, the fluidity of a conversation lends itself to explore areas where surveys can't go.[1] Again, by using an open interview style you can get valuable input to inform your strategy covering the whole customer life cycle. The goal of both techniques is to understand customers better; their behaviors, needs, goals and perceptions of the company, its competitors and industry

---

1 I will discuss the use of text data mining from social media and blogs to analyse customer input on brand and industry in its own section. I also have a section dedicated to statistical surveys.

both in the broadest business context as well as specifically where they interface with digital systems—and using one method does not exclude the other. Do both.

In addition to asking questions about markets, experiences and brands, customer interviews for digital strategy development should include device specific questions to get a better idea of what tasks are completed where. This may or may not deviate from general device use research, but during face-to-face sessions you can get valuable user scenarios attached to statistics to help you build business cases for specific changes to the digital ecosystem. However, if there are specific crucial business tasks you want customers to perform online, usability testing,[2] an analysis of how effective customers are at using your company's online assets, will be essential to make needed adjustments to optimize your systems. This could of course be conducted outside of interviews, but run in tandem they give insight into the differences between what people say and what they do. For instance you can discover the role your brand plays in shaping the customer experience. Often, if a person loves a brand, but is just having the hardest time getting through your overly clunky shopping cart, she might still say it was an okay experience. The opposite can be true if she dislikes the brand. Bottom line—emotions play on user sentiment.

Data privacy is another important area of questioning when interviewing customers. Find out what expectations your customers have about the safe keeping of their personal information and how much information are they willing to

---

2 In digital strategy, usability testing is used to uncover usability barriers in your digital system's present state or to test a work-in-progress to uncover issues that may prevent the accomplishment of online business goals but not to inform the interface design, although you could of course pair the tasks to save time and money.

give up so the system they visit will serve up relevant content to them. Customers and partners usually want a high level of relevancy and some level of recognition, but it is important to get a gauge for how much information they are willing to give in return. We accept that when logged into Amazon the system recognizes who we are and presents recommendations based on items previously bought, viewed or stored in shopping cart and other behavioral aspects of our past visits coupled with data on thousands of other people. Many news organizations now run software that will do the same when it comes to news content. I understand the publisher. They will increase their ad views if they hold visitors interested longer and they visit more pages, but are people interested in having their news habits tracked the same way as their shopping and travel history? Brands should stop and talk with their customers before they step over the line in the drive for relevance of content and ad optimization. Facebook is probably the best-known example of the negative pressure that can come from not talking to customers before changing such practices, with repeated uproar to their privacy policy changes as a consequence.

When it comes to the safe keeping of our data we assume everything is done to keep it away from unauthorized sources. If we trust the brand we do, but too often things get hacked. I got a letter from Adobe Systems in the winter of 2013 a few months after their systems got hacked as did probably many of you reading this. If they had interviewed me now I would have told them that I'm not happy. Not happy at all about having to check and double check everything moving forward to see if my identity has been stolen and if fraud has been conducted. But if they look at their customer data they will see no change—I need the "Creative Cloud" and "Acrobat Professional." That is a dangerous competitive position for a brand.

External stakeholders vary greatly from company-to-company and industry-to-industry and could include vendors, suppliers, business partners, investors, policy makers, media, etc. These stakeholders often have an intense and narrow focus on what you do and their input is often vital in shaping the content and functionalities targeted toward them. You will also need their input to build representative personas for use throughout the strategy process.

REVIEW OF AVAILABLE INFORMATION

This is a big messy bucket and the information needed should be defined as well as possible before it is poured out on the table for the team to sort through to avoid time wasted on misleading and unwanted information. The essential elements in "review of available information" are obvious and include the company's business strategy, related business unit strategies, brand strategy, marketing and communication plans, and proprietary and secondary industry research, surveys and studies. But it can also include website and social media content, case studies, published articles, news sources, product and service specific information, annual reports, sales projections, sale presentations, etc. The list is almost endless, so it is easy to see why it needs to be defined and limited to the pieces essential to creating the strategy to avoid information overload.

ONLINE MARKET OPPORTUNITY

The interviews and the study and review of company, products and industry should give your team a good idea of external stakeholders from customers to potential partners along with an understanding of the high-level topics that matter most to them. Armed with this information you start what is probably the most exciting and revealing task—searching for the online market opportunity. The size of your market online and the complexity of how to reach your audience will guide the scale and scope of your strategies.

There are many different ways to go about estimating, segmenting and rating the online market opportunity. If you are Gillette and you are marketing men's razors you could define your audience as every male from puberty and up. Then you could collect online statistics for every market you sell your product in and find how many are online, age groups, income, education, etc., and start targeting specific products and match them with behavioral data. This is a simplified account, but the point is that it becomes increasingly complex from here.

A good place to start is online search volume. That will give you an idea of the number of active seekers for your type of product or service. Interviews and the information review will have given you a long list of keywords and topics your stakeholders would care about in their hunt for solutions online. This list you can load into search engine planning tools to see monthly search volume by geographic regions. The search volume for any given product or solution shows a very direct market opportunity. If you are a herbal tea wholesaler wondering if you should open an online storefront and go direct-to-consumer it would be great to know that there are over 1.4 million tea-related searches on Google on average every month. It gives you a place to start your planning, but it does not show you the full potential of your online market opportunity.

To find the total opportunity you will often have to make an educated guess based on a series of data sources. Industry research can give you the total market, but rarely will it tell you how many are online and what their behavior is. Depending on the brand you are developing a strategy for you can get useful data from industry organizations, publication media kits, and social media membership data and review these with your own website analytics.

ONLINE ANALYTICS

Online analytics is the measurement, collection, analysis and reporting of internet data for purposes of understanding and optimizing your digital ecosystem. At the heart of the ecosystem is usually a brand's website since that often is the targeted destination for stakeholder conversion—be that sale, sign-up for a customer loyalty program, download of premium content that requires the submission of lead generating data, or accessing "member-only" content through a log-in. However, the landscape is ever changing and many of the goals mentioned above can also be handled on non-proprietary platforms.

Online analytics are used to analyze the traffic and usage patterns of a company's online assets with the goal of better understanding customer behavior online in order to identify strengths, weaknesses, opportunities, and threats to the company's current online offerings. This normally includes analytics from customer facing websites, employee sites, vendor portals, campaign sites, email delivery platforms, advertising campaigns, and social media pages and other online platforms. In addition to studying the data for the specific platforms, you should seek to glean insight into cross platform behavior. Our behavior online and the way we seek information is non-linear, but there are commonalities and patterns from search terms used to types of content that trigger specific actions.

If possible and if resources are available you should conduct the analysis of your digital ecosystem's online analytics in tandem with your sentiment analysis[3] or if you have the resources—a full analysis of available unstructured text data[4] generated by customers or other relevant stakeholders from sources such as social media, blogs, news media and customer service logs. The difference between the two methods of analysis is that the latter goes beyond sentiment to look for positive or negative trends for specific products and services. Studying traffic patterns and behavior such as the use of online functions and time spent with content next to a review of the tone of engagement or information exchange naturally complement each other. But the analysis of online analytics is extremely valuable on its own as well and a "must do" task in this process.

Funnel analysis is a specific methodology for web analytics where your company's online assets or digital ecosystem are viewed as a conversion funnel. A funnel analysis considers every visitor to an entry page in your ecosystem as a potential new lead or sale. Each of your online pages should be defined within your funnel. A YouTube video could be at the entry of

---

3 Sentiment analysis (also known as opinion mining) refers to the use of natural language processing, text analysis and computational linguistics to identify and extract subjective information in source materials. Generally speaking, sentiment analysis aims to determine the attitude of a speaker or a writer with respect to some topic or the overall contextual polarity of a piece of content. Source: Wikipedia.

4 Unstructured Data (or unstructured information) refers to information that either does not have a pre-defined data model or is not organized in a pre-defined manner. Unstructured information is typically text-heavy, but may also contain data such as dates, numbers, and facts.

the funnel while a content piece dealing with implementing or using your product and service could be towards the end. You define the conversion points depending on your strategic and business goals. Your online visitor hitting the purchase confirmation page or the follow button in LinkedIn could be considered conversions on the way to becoming a lead ready for your sales team or a direct online sale.

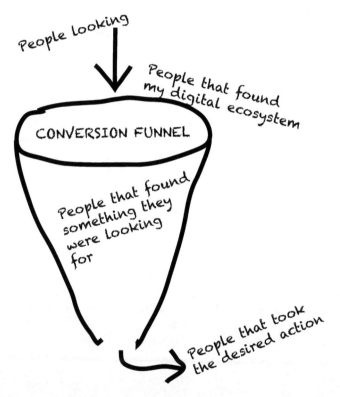

Figure 16.2   Conversion funnel

The goal of the analysis is to provide insight into how a traffic and content strategy can support the overall sales process, customer preference and brand loyalty, and identifying where in the conversion funnel the largest percentages of users drop and fixing the weak points and optimizing the overall conversion rate.

SENTIMENT ANALYSIS AND TREND MINING OF UNSTRUCTURED DATA—BIG DATA

Mining social media sites, blogs, consumer reviews and other such data sources help an organization find out what individual customers think and want. Equipped with these insights, it can then develop products and services for specific customer segments and craft more personalized marketing messages—as well as enhancing the brand. This may explain why three-quarter of CEOs say they're increasing their technology investments.

PwC 16th Annual Global CEO Survey, 2013

A manual sweep through the social sphere can provide a seasoned analyst with valuable insights, but to get a better read on a brand's standing among stakeholders software is used to crunch the data. Therefore, sentiment analysis or trend mining of online content are increasingly becoming an important part of strategy research. This is especially true for consumer brands or businesses and organizations that provide the infrastructure for our lives such as energy companies, the health sector and telecom, where the conversation volume generates enough data for proper analysis. Technically, sentiment analysis and trend mining refers to the use of software to harvest online text-based data, and in most cases it refers to social media and blogs, places where customers can comment and provide their opinion. Trend mining using multiple data sets are commonly referred to as big data.

Partner with a company that has the technology and the expertise to conduct natural language processing, text analysis and computational linguistics to identify and extract subjective information in the source material, but be aware that you have to tell the software what it needs to look for and how to rank what it finds. Your existing customer insight combined with a clear idea of what you are looking for are critical success factors.

We are in the middle of a project now for a TV network where the goal is to better align the future program mix and channel composition to what customers actually want and to set up a real-time performance measurement program to determine if decisions are on target. Our software partner in the project is one of the major players in the "big data" space, but without our client's and our input and know-how about the shows, such as actors names, show times and themes, along with targeted customer demographics and geographic differences, it would just be a load of text data collected by a great piece of software. It's the old adage—crap in crap out.

Generally speaking, sentiment analysis aims to determine the attitude of online voices with respect to what matters to your brand. The attitude may be his or her judgment or evaluation, the emotional state of people when writing, or the emotional affect the author wishes to have on the reader. Sentiment analysis combined with a strong survey methodology, and other relevant data can be a powerful tool to help shape your future customer-centric strategies.

FINANCIAL ANALYSIS OF SYSTEMS AND PROGRAMS

Financial analysis for the purposes of a digital strategy development can take many forms, but most commonly it refers to an analysis of a company's financial data with the goal of understanding the financial impact, positive and negative, that investments in digital systems, ongoing optimization changes to those systems, and the resources that run them will have on a company. With some systems such as shopping cart and check-out systems it is easy to see the correlation between investment and project financial impact, but in other areas it is less clear. If you are activating customer service in social media and are integrating the response software they use with Facebook or other solutions it can be more difficult to analyze positive or negative financial impact since "time-to-resolution" is a nebulous quantity.

Calculating customer lifetime value to arrive at a profitable new customer acquisition cost and customer retention cost can be vital to set-up marketing and sales programs with a return on investment. Working with the insurance industry put this into focus for me. They have such a clear grasp of such data because calculating risk and lifetime value against customer volume is part of how they price their products—extremely simplified. If they can acquire customers under a certain cost above a set volume they know that statistically that policy will be profitable for them. So when we devised online campaigns for the insurance industry we knew exactly what we could spend per lead since they had a clear projection on lead to close ratio from their experienced sales force. Not all industries have all this figured out, so in most processes this can be an important part of the facts and insights phase.

ANALYZE THE CURRENT SALES CYCLE AND SALES PROCESS

Much is said and written about "content marketing" lately. In the area of customer-focused business strategies it must be the number one buzzword next to "big data" with "loyalty" right behind. Analyzing the sales and purchase process is much about content marketing and loyalty strategies. If you understand how a product is bought and how it is best sold you will be able to tailor effective strategies.

You have acquired much of the qualitative and quantitative information that is needed to analyze and map out the sales cycle during the interviews and in the review of company data. Talking to the sales team provides good insight to sales processes, but sales, however, do not have all the answers. They will have some great ideas, but much is a description of business as usual and that is rarely good enough. Sales teams are often opinionated and will serve up their organizational myths as facts. That said, good sales people understand their customers and the information and assistance they must provide them with during the sales process regardless of whether this is selling shoes or power plants. Sometimes a sales team will be apprehensive, thinking that digital processes will take over some of the processes they own today, and they may be right, but in most instances a great sales force is essential, regardless of the quality of the digital strategy and its execution.

Figure 16.3   Customer life cycle

There is a general consensus about the main steps in a customer life cycle. The sales cycle to a great extent follows the same path—steps one through three—in the wheel above. The journey, whether it is a repeat purchase or first time around, starts with the feeling that there is a need to be met or a problem that should be solved followed by awareness that there is a product or service that can be purchased that can fill the need or solve the problem. After considering to pursue this product or service category the research of the possible solutions begins. Once the best options have been identified there will be an evaluation process for the optimal solution against pre-determined selection criteria. In the making a deal phase the relationship between customer and brand starts for real and often the tone of future interactions is set before the quick transaction of the actual purchase. In the period right after the purchase your buyer wants assurance that the right choice has been made. This multifaceted validation period along with the buyer's experience with the newly acquired product and service will color the loyalty phase and determine if you get an active or a passive brand advocate or someone who will never do business with you again.

The key to this process, however, is to get away from this generic wheel and create a narrative that is unique to the brand at hand. To create that narrative you need to develop personas or character sketches as described in the brand section. If the brand process is not a part of the digital strategy project you need to develop personas at this stage using the information gathered and analyzed at previous steps of the project. Often several personas compose the purchasing decision team— regardless of whether this is a B2B or B2C sales arena. Create "purchasing teams" to match different sales or needs/problem scenarios, and give each team member tasks from "hunter" or researcher to final decision maker. Then take your "hunter" and imagine a solution-gathering project. I prefer to visualize it as a timeline with a set team touch point where the hunter will present alternatives and candidates. Be honest as you study how you would perform on this timeline today and then set goals for how you would like to perform. The first step you must grapple with is: "Will I be found?" If your brand is not a household name or market leader in your industry you are not necessarily auto-selected for the sales process. I was in a meeting the other week with a newly appointed CEO for a large government-funded organization. This was a get to know each other session. During our discussion it came up that they had just engaged another consultancy for a project we would have been perfect for. It was not that he would not have wanted to work with us it was just that his team did not know that we also excelled at that area of management consulting. Lesson taken—we needed to optimize our online presence to match those services better. The next time we will

156

be one of the vendors partaking in their Request for Proposal (RFP) process.

If you are found you are among the companies being evaluated. This is the total group or 100 percent of the candidates. Where do you think the "hunter" found you? Your Wikipedia page, website, distributor's website, LinkedIn, Facebook, YouTube video? How are you positioned there? How do you lead him to other online properties? Will you today be in the percentage that is still in the running after the initial discovery of your company's online presence? Follow your persona-created sales team until purchase and then run another scenario with a new group of personas with a different "need/problem."

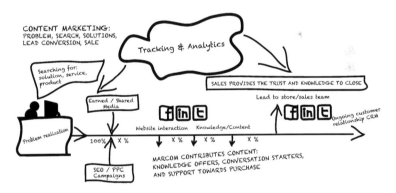

Figure 16.4   Consumer owned sales cycle drawing

I like to draw up a diagram similar to the one above. Complexity varies with the product or solution sold. A digital SLR camera is a hefty pro-sumer purchase and your average amateur photographer might spend anywhere from a weekend to months researching her next upgrade. If you sell power plants to governments, municipalities and utilities around the world your sales process could take years and contain a small library of content from statistical research to brand strengthening videos.

Customizing this diagram for your purposes is a great exercise to help your team visualize your customers' purchase processes. It requires an analysis of a customer's purchase behavior or service behavior that looks across all the different channels in which customers interact with a company's products or information. There are lots of different ways to do this. A representative example would be that a company focuses on the customer purchase process: how a customer becomes aware of a product, how a customer develops the intent to purchase a product, and how a customer actually purchases the product. The analysis looks at which channels, e.g. phone, catalog, retail store, social media, web site, 3rd party search engine, etc., a customer uses at what stage of the purchase process, and attempts to understand why each channel is used and evaluates the company's strengths or weaknesses in that particular channel for that particular stage of the process.

In addition it is good to look at post-purchase behavior: Do your customers come back to your site and:

- Rate the product

- Answer surveys

- Contact customer service

- Register product

- Recommend or otherwise connect on social media

RESEARCH, FACTS AND INSIGHTS (16)

- Sign up for newsletter or other news distributed through email.

Analyzing the sales process to create a starting point for your content marketing strategy is one thing, but you also need to look at goals and processes along the purchase timeline. Which data do we want and which data do we need to collect on our customers? How should we store this information? Who should have access to what information? How should leads be distributed and at what maturity? There are multiple variables here depending on the type of organization you are dealing with. In the travel industry you are dealing with a complex network of online resellers. Likewise for consumer goods, but in addition there are the brick and mortar stores. The car industry needs to get people away from their online research and into a dealership to test-drive a car. Business-to-business companies need to generate quality sales leads and support the sales cycle. And everyone is dealing with customer loyalty. An analysis of a company's CRM or customer databases and information repositories with the goal of segmenting customers into homogeneous groups across one or more dimension of behavior, demographics, value, product or marketing message affinity, etc. can belong in this process as well.

ONLINE AND OFFLINE COMPETITIVE ANALYSIS

Most companies have conducted competitive analyses for some aspects of their business, but rarely do I find that a thorough online competitive analysis has been performed. Every company wants to know how they stand and perform against their competitors and they should. As it relates to

digital, this requires conducting a thorough online analysis of all marketing and online campaigns, websites, social media pages, loyalty programs, customer service, retail environments, consumer facing software, etc.

In addition to your main competitors you should also look at new entries to your market place. They are often the ones that have disrupted or are going to disrupt your industry and are often where you will find radical innovation.

The goal of this process is to understand your company's strengths, weaknesses, opportunities, and threats as they stand now against established competitors, new market entries or disruptive technologies that could replace products and services you are offering.

While this process often includes steps found in traditional competitive analysis, such as products, prices, etc., a competitive analysis for developing your digital strategy includes three unique items:

- Benchmarking of the online ecosystem in relation to established competitors and new entries

  - A benchmark study conducted by a user interaction professional and a content expert who knows the industry or business area well

- Heuristic evaluation

  - An evaluation by a usability expert of the usability and user experience of a company's online assets compared and contrasted to those of its competitors and potential substitutes

- Features/functionality analysis

  - An evaluation of the features and functionality provided by a company's online assets, compared and contrasted with those of its competitors and potential substitutes.

For each of the areas covered in the competitive analysis I prefer to set up a numeric rating system based on a number of criteria relevant to the brand in addition to a descriptive evaluation. Even if the numeric rating process is highly subjective it will provide a score the brand can premeasure for improvements as the strategy is deployed.

ETHNOGRAPHIC RESEARCH

When it comes to ethnographic research for digital strategy development the focus is now on people's behavior in different environments with their handheld devices, stationary screens and screen tracking studies are less important now as best practices for web and mobile app design have clear guidelines to meet customer expectations, but they are still highly valued if you have a complex task performed by users online. Ethnographic research today analyzes customers' behavior in their environment, for example: field observations of shoppers in a store, travellers at an airport or visitors to a large convention or trade show and how they interact with their mobile devices or other available screens. We can use telecom data pared with transactional data and online traffic to get a quantitative view of mobile user patterns in stores and draw up strategies that will improve brand performance, but adding field studies can uncover patterns that can be vital to optimizing performance.

Most of us still carry our loyalty programs in our wallets in the form of cards with magnetic strips that we pull out at hotels, airports, rental car agencies, stores, etc. One thing is to study the data the programs generate, but you can learn a lot from observing the employee customer interaction to learn how we can improve services. I cannot remember a single incidence from the past year when I have been thanked at the hotel check-in or airport lounge for being a frequent customer. How hard can that be? Many brands are struggling to get maximum benefits out of their programs, feeling they are leaving money on the table. Implementing and running a loyalty program is costly if the return is not there. Studying people's actual behavior within program scenarios can provide valuable data for ongoing improvements.

In addition to standard ethnographic research, digital strategy may also include studying behavior within a specific social media platform, the video taping of customers using their computer or handheld devices or specific computer applications, web sites or social media platforms. As described earlier, we pair this with user interviews after the task has been completed, because we often find discrepancies between sentiment and actual task completion. Often this gap is created by brand preference. This insight will help you align your results.

STATISTICAL SURVEYS[5]

Surveys are a proven method for collecting quantitative and qualitative feedback from large groups. The tone and how you

---

5 Statistical surveys are undertaken with a view towards making statistical inferences about the population being studied, and this depends strongly on the survey questions used. Polls about public opinion, public health surveys, market research

compose your survey questions are crucial for your outcome and should be devised in such a manner that conclusions and trends can be drawn from the data you pool from your survey. In a digital strategy, surveys may be used to validate or invalidate key questions or assumptions raised in more qualitative exercises such as customer interviews and focus groups. Depending on the breadth of the survey population and the degree of variation within the population, survey results may be segmented to form homogeneous groups across one or more dimension of behavior, demographics, value, product or marketing message affinity, etc. Surveys are often conducted online using web intercepts, e-mail lists, or 3rd party panels, although phone surveys or other offline means may sometimes be used when there are doubts about the online savvy-ness of a particular target population.

TECHNICAL PERFORMANCE ASSESSMENT OF DIGITAL SYSTEMS

Performance assessment reviews the effectiveness of current digital tools and systems to discover barriers and define needs. But you should first outline the programs that will meet the needs of the business vision and conform to the business plan before you spend much time assessing existing and old systems. With your future systems outline and plan in hand you can conduct a gap analysis where the current technical architecture is assessed. Identify the gaps between the current

---

surveys, government surveys and censuses are all examples of quantitative research that use contemporary survey methodology to answer questions about a population. Although censuses do not include a "sample," they do include other aspects of survey methodology, like questionnaires, interviewers, and nonresponse follow-up techniques. Surveys provide important information for all kinds of public information and research fields, e.g., marketing research, psychology, health professionals and sociology. Source: Wikipedia.

state and future state, and outline initiatives and projects to fill those gaps. These initiatives should be sequenced and developed in order of their strategic importance.

ORGANIZATIONAL AND PROCESS ASSESSMENT

Similar to a technical performance assessment, organizational and process assessments look at the changes that need to be made in an organization and its processes in order to achieve the online vision. They may involve a series of business process reengineering projects focused on the areas of an organization most affected by online initiatives. An example is the training and organizational changes needed if customer service should start to respond to customer questions on Facebook. A form of gap analysis could be helpful here as well. Define your dream digital team, find the gaps and start hiring and training.

The results and plans for both your technical performance assessment of digital systems and your organizational and process assessment will become part of the digital governance structure.

⑰ Finally we're seeing the Big Picture through Big Data

If you look at all the data sets analyzed in this process, both qualitative and quantitative, this is what we commonly refer to as big data. Big data analysis from a marketing and customer insights perspective has a focus on how data sets play to the growth of the brand. Companies have other common uses for big data where data sets are analyzed with the intent to go "lean" or streamline supply chain or some of the many other business processes where large data sets can help leaders make better decisions. My focus is on big data analysis in regards to top-line growth including increased customer satisfaction and more cost optimized systems and programs. For this I analyze brand sentiment, customer behavior, industry performance, and system and program performance to solve problems, capture market opportunities and reduce risk.

Over eight hundred C-level executives responded to a McKinsey online survey conducted in 2013. The responses represented a full range of industries, regions, and company sizes and the results indicated growth in company-wide use of big data and advanced analytics. The results of this survey match what I am experiencing with companies of all stripes. Increasingly we see executives considering analytics of customer and consumer data a critical priority and dedicating increasing attention to the deployment of new analytic tools. In the McKinsey survey respondents reported increased use of data to improve decision-making, R&D processes, and budgeting and forecasting—and importantly, executives say their companies are using analytics to grow. The largest share of the study's respondents focus their analytics efforts on either increasing revenue or improving process quality; reducing costs tends to rank as a lower-level priority. Increasing revenue and improving process quality is precisely the purpose of developing a holistic digital strategy and a solid governance of the programs and systems.

For the purposes of breaking big data down into usable chunks for developing programs or systems as part of your company's digital strategy, an acknowledged methodology is the use of personas. Personas, as mentioned earlier, are data-built character sketches defined by gender, age, education, geographic location, etc. The approach is to create the personas based on the research and analysis conducted at the start of any strategy process such as customer interviews, ethnographic research, statistical surveys and the company's own user data.

Each persona represents a typical member of one customer or stakeholder segment and includes a short back-story and a needs/solution scenario along with demographic data and an illustrative image of the character as I have shown.

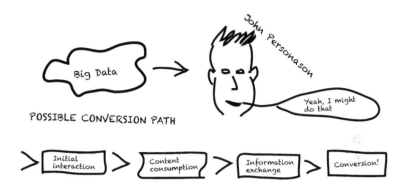

Figure 17.1 Conversion path

Personas are a framework for using customer information as the basis for decision-making. You essentially "ask" personas if a workflow, usability design or conversion path works for them.[1]

In addition, personas can effectively be used at high-level decision-making, kicking off brainstorming sessions, or virtual focus groups reviewing design comps[2] and campaign messaging. Because a persona represents a customer/stakeholder segment it allows decision makers to prioritize

---

1 A conversion path is the path that segments respondents to online advertising, search campaigns or other content sources, from the landing page to the desired action triggering the conversion. Conversion paths utilize user-directed segmentation, where a respondent is offered segmentation choices to make an act in their self-interest. After self-segmenting, users land on pages that deliver more tailored content and finally the pitch. Unlike a single landing page, a conversion path does not ask for a desired action, or a conversion, until a respondent has self-segmented. The conversion path is key to improve a web site's conversion rate. Source: Wikipedia.

2 In graphic design and advertising, a comprehensive layout or comprehensive, usually shortened to comp, is the page layout of a proposed design as initially presented by the designer to a client, showing the relative positions of text and illustrations before the final content of those elements has been decided upon. The comp thus serves as a draft of the final layout, and (if approved) is used as a guide for further design changes and, ultimately production. Source: Wikipedia.

goals, services and functions based on the needs of a specific personified segment. Because a persona is a character sketch, it is sometimes easier for decision makers to internalize the key needs of the segment than it would be by reading reams and reams of data.

(18) The Strategy Documents,[1] Campaigns and Builds

It is great to have a lot of information and insight, but ultimately the information needs to become an executable plan linked to business goals. To be truly worth anything to the organization this plan or digital strategy needs to take the company to a new level of digital maturity as defined by Cap Gemini and the MIT Sloan School of Management in their 2013 report *The Digital Advantage: How digital leaders outperform their peers in every industry*. In this report they define digital maturity as a combination of two separate, but related, dimensions.

The "first dimension", digital intensity, is investment in technology-enabled initiatives to change how a company

---

1 There is an overlap in documents defined as strategy documents, (as in outlining the company's digital strategy), governance documents, (as in detailing timelines, processes, guidelines and rules), campaigns, (as in specific tactics that are meant to further the strategy under the governance) and, finally, software or builds, (as in websites and applications where the strategy lives and is monitored day after day). The distinctions made in this book are for the purposes of the narrative.

operates—its customer engagements, internal operations, and even business models. As examples they pulled out Burberry and how they used technology to improve the in-store experience and increase operational excellence and Codelco's automation of their mining operations to improve efficiency and safety while creating new business opportunities to show that companies in all industries are investing in interesting digital initiatives.

However, in many organizations, these investments are uncoordinated and sometimes duplicative. They go on to state that firms maturing in the "second dimension", transformation of management intensity, are creating the leadership capabilities necessary to drive digital transformation in the organization. Transformation intensity consists of the vision to shape a new future with the governance and engagement to steer the course, and IT/business relationships to implement technology based change. As examples of transformation management intensity the report presents case studies of Volvo that developed a vision and governance capabilities before it began to implement new digital services in its cars and of Nike building a digital division called Nike Digital Sport to coordinate and extend the successful activities it had built separately in social media, digital product design, custom manufacturing, and other areas. The elements of transformation management intensity work together— through a combination of top-down leadership and bottom-up innovation—to drive ongoing digital transformation. However, in many companies, these elements are overly slow or conservative, preventing the company from investing in innovative opportunities.

Therefore it is paramount that company leadership is well represented and takes ownership of formulating the digital strategy. A 2013 study by McKinsey shows a trend of higher involvement from the c-suite (CEO, CFO, COO, etc.) in digital strategy initiatives. Growing shares of respondents reported that their companies' senior executives are now supporting and getting involved in digital initiatives. In 2013, 31 percent say their CEOs personally sponsor these initiatives, up from 23 percent who said so in 2012. This growth illustrates the importance of these new digital programs for corporate performance, as well as the conundrum that many organizations face: often, the CEO is the only executive who has the mandate and ability to drive such crosscutting programs that a holistic digital strategy represents.

Usually a strategy process sets the course for 36 to 60 months, so at the time of conception it should be ahead of its time and still function excellently in the present. To do this the strategy must be agile and flexible. The team needs to make the company stretch, but not commit to something that is unrealistic for the organization to implement or maintain both in relation to budgets and resources. You can train and you can hire but you can't change an organization overnight.

A digital strategy is often written as a two-step process as described earlier. First a simplified business case is presented. The simplified case should have enough data to verify its recommendations, but written in a language that makes it easy for leadership to understand what they are giving the green light to. The main goal of the simplified business case is to show the benefits the plan will have for the company in achieving its business goals and why the total investment is worth doing. The simplified business case also presents the key performance indicators (KPIs) that will be used to measure and evaluate the success of the online strategy. The quantitative definition of the KPIs comes in the full business case. For most processes

I've been involved in, the simplified business case incorporates three documents: a full text-based version, a pre-read and a slide-deck for presentation to top management.

With an approved, simplified business case as the steering document most companies divide up the areas that need to be developed or re-aligned. Depending on the size of the organization, developing the full business case can be a very involved process and many companies choose to attack business areas in progression. This will save your company the burden of having too many resources tied down in a planning process at the same time. With this approach to building the full business case you can develop plans for areas such as website, social media, loyalty programs, ecommerce, etc. based on the benefits it will bring to your organization. These sections will be further broken down and prioritized in the portfolio management process. Portfolio management is a way of prioritizing various initiatives by comparing their cost of implementation with their expected business benefits.

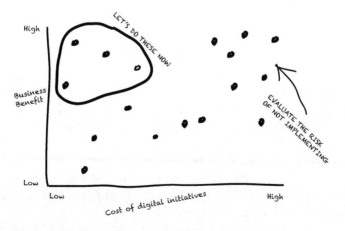

Figure 18.1   Portfolio management

Portfolio management is often done by creating a two by two matrix where cost of implementation runs along the x-axis (from high cost to low cost) and expected business benefit runs along the y-axis, from low benefit to high benefit. Individual initiatives or projects are then plotted on the matrix in terms of their calculated costs and benefits and priorities are determined according to which projects will provide the greatest benefit with the least investment.

The full business case for each of your business areas should consist of a complete and detailed text-based version with accompanying spreadsheets used to give a clear view of the total cost of implementation and the running of the programs on an ongoing basis including supplier and vendor estimates. Since corporate decision makers are often not well versed in the areas digital strategy touches upon and may find some of the tactics described difficult to understand, a visual proof-of-concept or graphical representations (comps) of key ideas and processes are part of the digital strategy and often presented as part of the simplified or full business plan to better explain the concepts within the plan to your internal audience or team. A visual proof-of-concept is often created in order to better communicate a key concept or to build excitement among stakeholders when building a consensus, getting estimates, budget approval, or socializing a digital strategy for a company-wide buy-in.

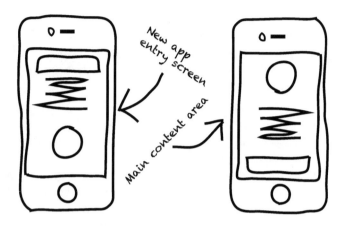

Figure 18.2   Proof of concept

VISUAL PROOF OF CONCEPT

Information architecture, wireframes and user interface designs are common sets of graphic representations of ideas for websites, social media, applications and software in general, and also represent a visualization of concept even if they are more technical in nature. The information architecture visualizes the content and the hierarchy it is presented in. Wireframes outline how content is presented on a page and the navigation structure. The interface design shows how a user would interact with the content. For some audiences this set of graphics can be black lines on white, but to excite many, go the extra step and design them to look like a finished product. Sometimes this makes buy-in easier, but the danger could be that discussion turns to color choices and not the essence of the concept.

While the information architecture shows the content areas for one specific platform within a holistic strategy, the content marketing strategy details how content and traffic will play across all platforms, how it benefits the brand, the sales cycle and other prescribed business goals. The content marketing strategy will often be synchronized with new product releases and include campaigns and media plans. With the fragmented media picture, spreading a brand's targeted audience across multiple platforms, content marketing has become a focal point for many companies seeking to build brand through engagement, or rather, in an information exchange with their customers and other stakeholders. To that effect an ongoing online media plan detailing the allocation of media spending across platforms to drive traffic to relevant content is often seen as part of the customer acquisition or retention portions of the digital strategy. Platforms included are normally search engine marketing, banner advertising, social media advertising, external email list acquisition, online affiliate networks and increasingly native advertising.[2]

This progressive approach to digital strategy builds a set of documents that quantifies opportunities and risks and investments and returns over time for the total digital ecosystem, and in my experience is an essential approach to moving from facts and insights and a business case to real-life implementation. The full business case for a company's total set of digital initiatives can be too much to get your head around at once. So even though a digital strategy

---

2 Native advertising is a web advertising method in which the advertiser attempts to gain attention by providing content in the context of the user's experience. Native ad formats match both the form and the function of the user experience in which it is placed. One form of native advertising, publisher-produced brand content, is similar in concept to a traditional advertorial, which is a paid placement attempting to look like an article. A native ad tends to be more obviously an ad than most advertorials. The advertiser's intent is to make the paid advertising feel less intrusive and thus increase the likelihood users will click on it. Source: Wikipedia.

development project provides the opportunity for a holistic approach it can be a key success factor in many instances to prioritize the business goals to keep the strategy process focused. For example, a digital strategy project may have a sales focus including customer acquisition and retention. In such a strategy you will look at all possible customer touch points and the internal resources, processes and tools needed to maximize their return for the customer and the company. The process pursued to develop such a digital strategy may for instance touch on supply chain, partner affiliates and human resources, but since that is not the main objective of the project, a complete analysis of these areas may in most cases not be needed.

The processes that will run and manage your digital strategy such as project plans, road maps, editorial calendars, measurement plan, ownership structure, guidelines, etc. will be dealt with in the next sections—getting started and digital governance.

PART V

Getting Started

(19) Setting Objectives: Stakeholders and their Requirements

For your digital strategy and governance to be successful, it is important to understand who your stakeholders are and what their specific requirements and drivers are so that the ongoing data analyses, performance measurements and reports will be meaningful to them. It is your stakeholder's goals that drive the business so there must be a clear understanding of governance responsibilities—meeting strategy, managing risks, allocating resources, delivering value and measuring performance.

For the purposes of digital strategy and governance, I have divided stakeholders into two groups—owners and managers—and outlined some of their measurement interests and requirements.

Owners—your business management team. Corporate leadership provides the funding and therefore has a vested interest in the success of your digital strategy and an ongoing concern that governance is met. They want to see a return on their investment and that there is an alignment with their total set of strategic objectives for their business. In addition to meeting and exceeding market opportunities your leadership wants to be assured that risk is monitored, that you are in compliance with corporate ethical standards, that you meet regulatory and legal requirements globally, and that corporate reputation is managed.

Here are some other top-level concerns the "owners" want as part of the reports they receive:

- Financial—ROI, profit and loss, cost v. budget, productivity, benefits realization, investments in improvements

- Customer—satisfaction, growth, upsell and more-sell, service, loyalty, quantitative and qualitative feedback (subjective as well as objective), strategic objectives v. actual projects/activities, reputation management, compliance with legislation and privacy regulations

- Process—capability benchmark, performance exceptions, transformation capability and tactical agility

- Learning—innovation, product development, product mix optimization, sales-cycle improvement, employee attrition, retention, skill profile, resource shortfall, training and development, risk identification and risk prevention.

Managers—run the programs and systems and include line management, staff and their suppliers—they need to meet "owner's" expectations and deliver in an efficient and effective manner on the digital strategy.

Here are some other top-level concerns the "managers" want as part of the reports they receive:

- Financial—Performance data analysis on strategic goals, sales, operational and project costs, cost allocation/ recovery, cost optimization

- Customer—Performance data analysis on strategic goals, quantitative and qualitative feedback from the digital system on brand, products and services (subjective as well as objective), customer retention and growth statistics, and the effectiveness of dealing with customer loyalty

- Process—Performance data analysis on strategic goals, internal improvement in efficiency and risk reduction, internal v. outsource support

- Learning—Performance data analysis on strategic goals, capability to deliver, readiness for new requirements, time to market for new initiatives, products and services, people and skills.

With these reporting needs in mind a key characteristic of any successful initiative is the establishment of an enterprise-wide approach that clearly sets out roles and responsibilities, emphasizing that everyone has a part to play in enabling successful outcomes.

The *owners* have the authority to make things happen and must give direction backed up with adequate support and sponsorship so that *managers* can realistically balance requirements with available resources, and if required, make additional resources available. It is vital that the *owners* insist on and seek measurable benefit to the organization and include the digital strategic objectives in their existing performance measurement program. In many companies only top management can implement cross business unit programs including coordination of overseas and satellite parts of the enterprise and ensure their interests and constraints have been considered. To do so *owners* must create an organization and structure that ensures broad involvement in the governance process—by forming cross business units committees and reporting processes, actively monitoring performance and risks, and effectively and resolutely correcting deviations from plan.

The *owners* recruit *managers* to run the systems and programs and give them a mandate to build an organization and the necessary infrastructure for successful execution. This mandate is important for the *managers* to take ownership of all the requirements of the programs and champion and foster collaboration across business units for digital governance activities. To anchor their mandate within the organization *managers* should build and achieve a pilot to verify the business case for their programs. The pilot will also enable your *managers* to define a control framework because it is important that *managers* set the direction for digital governance activities.

Your *managers* should also handle the practicalities to ensure that business strategy and objectives are set, communicated and aligned, and assess ongoing impact and risks. It is also their responsibility to establish reporting processes meaningful to stakeholders, communicate any business concerns in a balanced and reasoned way, and regularly check actual results against original or changed goals. Identifying critical processes and concerns, assessing risks and capability, and identifying gaps should also be part of the report to senior management as part of a performance measurement system.

For programs that demand internal organizational change, processes that clearly deviate from existing skillsets or require new ones to be adopted, *managers* should strive to nominate project champions who can create enthusiasm and sow the seeds of change within the affected teams. They should also assign the responsibility for quality assurance (QA) programs to individuals with the ability to provide constructive feedback to internal and external providers as part of a continuous improvement program. Ideally these people should also oversee and respond to QA feedback from customers and develop business cases for improvements if warranted and work with the *manager* to design, implement and commit skilled resources for these improvements and new solutions.

To run successful programs *managers* should foster support from internal and external specialist teams:

- IT: scope audits in coordination with governance strategy, provide assurance on the control over digital systems and platforms and provide assurance on the control over the digital performance management system

- Risk management: ensure that new risks are identified in a timely manner and provide advice towards resolution if needed

- Compliance officers: ensure that the digital ecosystem complies with policy, laws and regulations

- Finance: advise on and monitor costs and benefits, provide support for management information reporting, and incorporate governance requirements into purchasing and contract processes.

Accountability for achieving targets should be clear along with the ownership and collection of measurement data and the reporting process. The governance of performance measurement, as described in detail later in the book, should be formalized in service descriptions written in a language and using terms meaningful to the people involved. For third party service providers, on mission critical systems, a service level agreement (SLA) should form part of the contractual agreement so that performance measurement can be backed up with contractual recourse in the event of performance failure.

Implementing digital strategy for many organizations will mean major changes and therefore it is important to have high-level sponsorship and the active involvement of key stakeholders. Digital strategy has an iterative lifecycle that begins with an initial phase to define overall goals and to gain the support and commitment of top management that then leads to the ongoing effective governance of digital activities.

To get started it is beneficial that all teams and key stakeholders are identified, engaged and actively involved, including corporate leadership. Together they should define the meaning of governance in the organization and where digital governance fits in or if it is warranted as a stand-alone governance program. For most organizations it will be easier to manage that way. In the same initial process the teams should agree on a set of initial objectives. These initial objectives will define some of the success criteria for the initial phase of the digital strategies and the governance of the systems and programs. Along the same lines your team should identify organizational, environmental, or cultural constraints and enablers. These steps should be taken in conjunction with an initial gap analysis against industry best practice—if information is available—to demonstrate where digital programs are performing to plan and governance is already in place. This will highlight areas of focus for the implementation roadmap and give stakeholders an understanding of the expectations and restrictions and, properly communicated, achieve a broad understanding of the digital strategy and governance issues and benefits across all stakeholders.

Here are some points to consider:

- Agree to: publish and gain acceptance of an initial digital strategy and governance framework, tools and processes

- Creation of a project plan with definition and prioritization of the initial project deliverables

- Identification and commitment of the resources required to deliver initial projects

- Identification and sign-off of key performance indicators and critical success factors for this project

- Documented estimated timescales and resource implications as well as expected ROI

- Alignment with business objectives and strategy

- Identify some initial "quick wins" and have them implemented—to make digital strategy and governance "real" for your organization

- Acceptance of the published digital strategy and governance framework by those responsible for implementation

- An effective communication plan—who to, what, when etc. to overcome any barriers and to motivate change

- Current key projects mapped against governance plan, to look for easy fit/implications

- Ensure that changes are sustainable and can be institutionalized, i.e. become business-as-usual practices.

Armed with your full business case ready and signed off you are ready for implementation.

⟨20⟩ Defining your Digital Ecosystem

For many brands their digital ecosystem has grown organically since they launched their first website or social media page and often digital strategy is as much about taking down and stripping out as it is about building new. Many marketing and communications teams are surprised at what they find when they start digging, sites nobody has log-ins to anymore, a sales team in India has a Facebook page with the old logo, someone in product development has an active LinkedIn group, a blog was started as part of an advertising campaign two years ago with two irrelevant posts. Not only is this bad for the brand, but it exposes the company and the brand to unnecessary risk.

I am not advocating to ban initiative and creative thinking within an organization and disallow exploration in the digital realm, but this needs to be conducted within a governance structure where passwords are stored, policies and brand guidelines are followed, and where the company does not pay for redundant traffic or bids against itself on Google AdWords. Most importantly though, you must not confuse your customer. That can happen in many ways: your campaign site log-in is not integrated with company CRM, angering customers with established accounts who do not understand why their sign-in is refused, you are giving conflicting information in duplicated content, or the site has remained live after the campaign is over and the occasional visitor is left dazed and confused by the outdated content, tone and style.

To deal with an overgrown digital ecosystem you must do the detective work of finding all sites and social media pages, locate their owners, hosts, partners, and passwords, and then shut down those that are outdated and inactive as well as places without a business purpose. If you have nurtured relationships with people at the social media sales offices in your country they can often become your ally in getting pages closed that you no longer have access too or were opened maliciously by an outside party. Take the remainder of web, blog and social media sites you want to keep and place them in a diagram as depicted below where you can look at the interaction between sites and pages. I prefer to view the ecosystem in a frame divided based on functionality: open, closed, sender based or dialog based. With your sites and pages drawn on the whiteboard, this is a good way to start a creative and strategic brainstorming session with your team. Start to ask questions like:

- To where should we drive traffic?

- Which site and pages have a natural symbiotic relationship?

- Do we have the right resources for managing these platforms?

- Where are we seeing results according to plan?

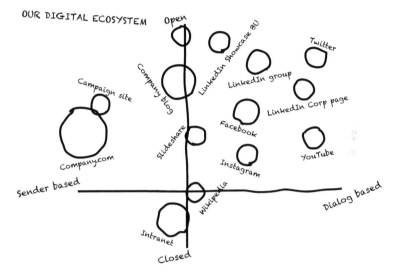

Figure 20.1 Digital ecosystem

Not every channel, system or program needs to be everything to everyone. It is time for your core work group to get down to the details of your online presence. Armed with the ecosystem diagram, your personas and the research from your strategy phase, refocus your core team from the big picture questions to specifics for each page. A good tool for this exercise is the type of matrix shown below. With the sites and channels on one side of the matrix and your brand's goals and ambitions on the other, your team will have a checklist as a framework to think through and discuss each program in your digital ecosystem. Your Twitter channel may currently be controlled by your media relations team and used solely to post notices on press releases with links back to the newsroom on your corporate website without using hash tags.

- Should we reply to tweets relevant to us by relevant stakeholders?

- Should we post links to knowledge-sharing content we create?

- Should we advertise and build our followers?

- Where do we direct our links to promote our point-of-view?

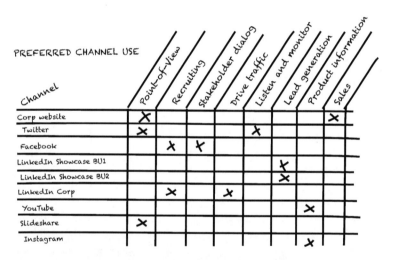

PREFERRED CHANNEL USE

Channel	Point-of-View	Recruiting	Stakeholder dialog	Drive traffic	Listen and monitor	Lead generation	Product information	Sales
Corp website	X						X	
Twitter	X				X			
Facebook		X	X					
LinkedIn Showcase BU1						X		
LinkedIn Showcase BU2						X		
LinkedIn Corp		X		X				
YouTube						X		
Slideshare	X							
Instagram							X	

Figure 20.2 Preferred channel use

The final "preferred channel use" matrix and the digital ecosystem diagram become part of your governance information and your performance measurement plan to make sure your teams are on plan. Of course, nothing should be set in stone and protected from further tweaks as the landscapes change. Eliminations and additions should be done as part of the ongoing performance measurement program described in the governance section of this book.

While the matrix above is a good workshop exercise to get the team thinking about what they want each platform to do and what you can realistically accomplish within each channel's format and target audience composition, a one page summary of the page objectives works well for leadership buy-in and "sign-off." Below is a sample one pager created for an energy company.

Twitter handle: @company_name

Primary purpose: Point-of-view—**direct traffic to non-owned channels**

Secondary purpose: Point-of-view—**direct traffic to owned channels**

Tertiary purpose: Participate in dialog

Geographic reach: One global account.

Business area strategy: Object is to tell our point-of-view on stories people already follow on global, national, regional, and business area issues through a hash-tag/multi-hash-tag strategy. Target audience—tier one stakeholders:

- Shareholders and the financial market (capital and insurance providers)

- Employees and their representatives (current and prospective)
- Authorities (home and host governments, legislators/ politicians, regulators and administrative bodies at global/regional/national/local levels)
- Next generation elites (likely upcoming decision makers in the political, business and/or civil society sphere that may have a direct or indirect influence on our activities).

Target audience—tier two stakeholders:

- The "public" (whether the general public in countries of operation, host communities neighboring our operations, or individual "activists" that mobilize across boundaries and borders)
- Opinion leaders (stakeholders, typically in positions of indirect influence, that have a disproportionate leverage on opinions, whether in the financial, political, industry-specific or civil society realms)
- Media (in countries of operation and international)
- Non-governmental associations and civil society organizations.

Dialog and engagement: Correct facts, answer direct questions.

(21) An Honest Evaluation of your People and Systems

Measuring and evaluating people's skillsets and the technology they have bought and implemented is a sensitive but necessary task. Because of internal political sensitivity, consultants are often brought in to do this task. This brings to mind scenes like the classic "I have people skills, damn it!" clip from Mike Judge's *Office Space* where consultants Bob and Bob are tasked with evaluating the resources of the fictive software company Innotech. Check it out on YouTube and then know that reality is not quite like that—at least not in my world. Most of the time the companies we deal with and the people involved know that they have a shortage of digital expertise. In a 2013 survey by McKinsey, *Bullish on Digital*, 17 percent of CEOs cited lack of available talent as the factor for failure of digital initiatives. Pair that with the 2013 CMO survey[1] where 80 percent of the respondents plan to increase their digital marketing spend with an average of 10 percent. It is clear that the supply of talent is not keeping up with

---

1 Conducted annually by The CMO Survey.org.

demand and the more complex the task or strategy that needs to be implemented the smaller the pool is to choose from. Gone are the days when management thought digital talent was anyone under 25 and that simply being online gave you expertise. No joke. I remember those days.

The surveys quoted above and other assessments carried out around the world have shown that in general, digital capabilities have not kept pace with increasing online opportunities and subsequent exposure to risk. Because of this high demand, digital is for many employees an area they want to and strive to transition into. That is good, but they need training and education. In addition, the rapid pace of change often leaves existing teams behind if the company does not have adequate training programs. A digital strategy without a governance plan with a strong emphasis on ongoing education and training is bound to fail or not even get off the ground. I have spent countless hours training teams from C-level to line staff and it is rewarding both ways. Noone learns more than the teacher.

In many organizations top-level management have an unclear view of their digital capability and find it very difficult to understand the technical and organizational environment upon which they increasingly depend. Often inadequacies only manifest themselves when projects fail, costs spiral, operational systems crash, or service providers fail to deliver the promised value. Reacting after the fact is not how anyone wants to manage their business and besides, it exposes the company to financial and reputational risk. Monitoring and assessing the strength and quality of digital resources (people, applications, technology, facilities, UX, design, content, distribution, data, analytics) to ensure that they are capable of supporting the current and proposed digital strategy is a key aspect for the success of digital programs.

Instead of being the clean-up crew after a disaster your senior management should exercise sufficient governance and oversight. They should insist on objective and regular assessments of their internal and external providers of digital programs and the systems that run them to ensure that major problems are exposed. The capability assessment should be followed by the necessary action to rectify shortfalls in the programs through upgrades, process change, training or hires. Agreement must be reached regarding where and how to address inadequacies, by investing in the internal infrastructure, seeking externally provided outsourced resources, or by accepting the risks of not adequately meeting today's and future demands. Cost control and reducing inefficiencies are also important reasons for reviewing your systems and programs and your people's capability. Improving your company's level of digital capability and the maturity in which the organization handles its digital programs both reduces risks and increases productivity and in most cases— profit.

—— 0 ——

Companies of all sizes and across all industries are now facing a massive digital disruption that will permeate their cores. Information technology has been working its way into business processes for decades, but this is different: The apps, data and APIs that are driving this digital transformation are not just enabling business; they are becoming its very fabric.

Promod Haque, Senior managing partner, Norwest Venture Partners

With digital programs and processes becoming the very fabric of business the key to a successful digital performance is to make sure your company makes the right investments and orchestrate an optimal use and allocation of people, applications and technology. In the optimization of resources, IT plays a central role, but equally important is your business-centric data analysis team. Both will increasingly service needs from the whole company. Also, you must build up the digital expertise in your key business teams such as sales, marketing, human resources, and customer service, or find an optimal way for these teams to share resources. When it comes to optimizing your software and hardware or system investments, most corporations tend to focus on the planning and acquisition of new systems instead of maximizing the efficiency of their existing digital assets and optimizing the costs relating to these assets—often due to weak ongoing performance measurement programs—so improvements have to be done in leaps rather than tweaks. Many are stuck in this costly iterative circle of constant implementation of new systems. Hopefully, with the emergence of enterprise cloud services smart companies can license less disruptive and costly solutions.

In regards to investments in both systems and people, leadership needs to address strategy, creativity, design, and infrastructure by ensuring that the planned benefits accruing from digital programs are real and achievable. Certain factors must be in place for this culture to develop:

- All digital programs have clear business objectives that are understood and measured.

- The responsibilities with respect to digital programs are understood and applied.

- Appropriate methods and adequate skills exist to manage and support digital projects and systems.

- Improved workforce planning and investment to ensure recruitment and, more importantly, retention of skilled staff.

- Digital programs education, training and development needs are fully identified and addressed for all staff.

- Appropriate facilities are provided and time is available for staff to develop the skills they need.

- Process, plans and support are in place for outsourcing programs and the use of partners and contractors.

- Appropriate methods and adequate skills exist in the organization to manage digital programs.

Digital assets and programs are complex to manage and continually change due to the nature of technology and changing business requirements. Effective management of the lifecycle of programs including hardware, software licenses, service contracts, and permanent and contracted human resources is a critical success factor in not only optimizing the digital cost base, but also for managing changes, minimizing service incidents, assuring a reliable quality of service, and maximizing opportunities and earnings from the programs.

Of all the digital assets, human resources represent the biggest part of the cost base and on a unit basis the one most likely to increase. Identifying and anticipating the required core competencies in the workforce is therefore essential. When these are understood, an effective recruitment, retention and training program is necessary to ensure that the organization has the skills to utilize digital opportunities effectively in order to achieve the stated objectives.

To ensure that digital resources are managed effectively, capability should be assessed on a regular basis and whenever specialized resources are critical to strategic digital decisions the capability assessment and your required actions to meet proposed plans or changes should be based on an alignment of digital goals with business goals. Some of the things you should look at are:

- Assess your current capability for critical processes

- Determine the additional required capabilities and analyze any gaps

- Define and justify necessary improvement projects or hires

- Re-adjust the digital strategy by adjusting goals and improving capability, and outsource when cost-effective or to secure the required talents faster

- Provide transparent visibility of your company's capability position to those involved and affected.

In your efforts to be transparent and fair to the people concerned it is vital that communication is clear and support is provided for those that feel negatively affected. The danger with transparency is that people can misunderstand the information and take it as a personal attack if it relates to them, their group or the system and programs they run, have built or bought. Naturally, people fear for their jobs and their careers. This fear is heightened if resource evaluation is an ad hoc process run at times of cost cutting or other major changes. But if the organization places the resource evaluation process in an ongoing measurement program and conducts it with a regular frequency it can become a more natural and wanted part of management—and cause less disruption to your organization.

Regardless, the measurement of digital capability should be an objective assessment oriented towards business requirements. This will ensure that the current "as-is" and required "to-be" capabilities are realistic and measurable, enabling any gaps to be identified and a plan to be drawn up to rectify any shortcomings. With such a defined process, changes are more easily adapted by the organization.

The following principles are recommended when carrying out a capability assessment:

- Set Scope

- Use an acceptable measurement methodology agreed upon with the stakeholders and which is defined and transparent

- Set a baseline and present the "current state assessment" using a scale or rating system

- Set reasonable objectives for the targeted level of capability

- Define measures that relate both to "the journey" as well as the "end goal"

- Limit the number of measures, minimize measurement overhead, and avoid information overload.

Consider the following critical success factors:

- Appropriate level of ownership

- Avoid complexity and be flexible

- Embed measures into business-as-usual processes

- Ensure staff has adequate skills, training and tools

- Create a repeatable process and agree to frequency of reporting.

The real value of a capability assessment comes from the identification and implementation of cost-effective improvements of programs and training and hire of talent. A realistic and practical approach is required to ensure that the proposed changes are based on business priorities, will be supported and funded by management, and will be successfully implemented. A critical success factor is to understand your total environment: business, technology, data, and people. It also helps to establish support for your plan or capability improvement framework before you recommend changes. This will ensure your team that this will be an ongoing process and not a one-off project to fix the current and immediate gap. Your plan should set realistic targets and respond quickly and openly to environment changes. Stagger and prioritize your proposed improvements so the company can move quickly on what is most business critical and beneficial, and make sure that what you propose is achievable and has economically sound solutions that are scalable.

After you have successfully initiated a capability assessment approach, and perhaps performed a pilot project, a capability assessment process needs to be implemented as part of your normal business procedures. To reduce resistance within your organization clearly describe the effect on the business of the current capability state of affairs. Identify the ramifications of NOT improving capability, e.g. additional costs or risks, inability to realize opportunities, late or non-delivery of the strategic development program, redundant effort, loss of talent, etc. Articulate this current state of capabilities in a language people can understand in relation to your strategy, and describe for each specific area the benefits of implementing your planned improvements. It will also help if knowledge and data are available to benchmark levels of capability in the context of external comparisons. Finally, describe the projected effect on the business after the delivery and implementation of enhancements.

To help sustain capability enhancements you must agree on steering and review mechanism and identify the sponsors from line management to top management. There should be a prioritized program of improvements in place based on business benefits, and the capability assessment program should look for continuous improvement opportunities where improvement is relevant. Periodically review the objectives and reset goals if necessary, by checking the validity of goals against business strategy. All improvements must be achievable, sustainable, and relevant thereby increasing your success rate. Publish and celebrate successes to keep your teams motivated. Periodically, or in the case of milestone successes, communication to stakeholders and sponsors as well as the wider community could be warranted where there is likely to be a general interest in outcomes or if it is a genuine positive public relations opportunity.

(22) Communication and Change Management

Digital strategy is about improving the business environment and results from your digital programs whether this may be increased revenues, customer loyalty, product innovation or other factors. Improvement often implies change and in the fast moving digital realm change is inevitable. Everybody knows this, but still I cannot count the meetings I've been in where I can feel the reluctance to change as a physical presence. In such meetings many promising strategies die. It is a tough decision for management to take change head on when there is so much uncertainty about the road ahead, but when strategies get killed due to fear of change this becomes part of a corporate culture. That culture can become devastating. Business people are tossing out their Blackberrys and replacing them with Apple and Samsung phones. Everybody under 40 has a Gmail or Yahoo email account and not AOL accounts. The best electrical cars are made in Silicon Valley and not Detroit.[1] There can be massive market shifts harbored in your company culture between innovation and

---

[1] The outcome from the cases of exploding Tesla batteries has not materialized as of the writing of this book.

change and fear and stagnation. These are significant and much talked about cases from recent history, but if you look around in your industry I am sure there are plenty of stories where a culture's unwillingness to change has created market share losses. Dealing with development and implementation of digital strategy I see the fear and the complications of change all the time, but I also get to experience the wins in partnership with brave and innovative companies.

Throughout this book I have emphasized the importance of anchoring the digital strategy process within the organization from the development of the business case through implementation. Top management—as discussed—are a crucial success factor, but you need understanding, willingness and—if you can achieve it—excitement throughout the organization as well. This can be achieved through well-executed pilot programs. Pilots with positive and interesting results are a good way to get people's attention, but you will need more than their attention. At the heart of the organizational change forced through by implementation of new digital strategies are better processes, controls, training, best practices, and new management techniques. Now you are touching the inner fabric of your organization and your improvements will only have a chance of succeeding in a sustainable way if the culture of the organization is changed to drive and support the desired new management approach.

Effective communications are a key enabler of these changes, just as poor communications can create a legacy of misunderstanding, lack of trust, and technical mystique and hype in many organizations. I have seen it in practice many times—more often earlier in the century—where the head of IT could kill an idea with a buzzword that would have everyone shaking their heads in silence until someone changed the subject. In the period from 1995 to 2005 I was often brought in as a translator or bridge between teams since I spoke three languages: "digital," "business" and "marketing." I learned a tremendous amount from those meetings and the experience is invaluable to communicate and implement change across a business.

Keep in mind when you communicate change that if it is difficult to understand for those literate in digital strategy and governance practices and relatively close to the systems and programs in play, then it is even worse for the employee who finds technical jargon a smokescreen and the lack of information relevant to his or her business a major headache to deal with. Communication and cultural behavior, based on appropriate influencing strategies, are therefore key ingredients in any digital strategy program.

Given the significance of digital programs both in terms of investment and potential impact on the business—the risks of failing to exploit the potential digital programs for your strategic advantage must be stressed in all communication about digital strategy and governance programs implemented to run and monitor them. Wake-up calls are sometimes required at the highest levels. Stakeholders must understand and feel responsible for capturing opportunities and for safeguarding against risks.

—— 0 ——

When developing your communications plan you must consider who needs to be informed and what behaviors or attitudes need to be changed. It is important to remember that different messages are needed for different stakeholders and that the language used must be understandable, seem relevant

to the intended audience, and motivate positive attitudes to the changes and change process. Identifying and gaining the support of internal opinion leaders can be paramount in many organizations. These people are not necessarily part of management or leadership, but are employees that have the respect of their peers and are considered experts in their fields. This could be a young marketer running the social media programs, an experienced engineer in the IT team or a sales superstar. These are key influencers who can make or break an effective roll-out, but it is also vital to recognize the main stakeholders impacted by the change. These are the ones who are getting handed a new set of KPIs for themselves and their teams. They may have fears that are not directly related to the strategy implementation, but that nevertheless affect them personally, such as bonus structures, reporting structures, job titles, and promotion paths. Find how you want to influence particular stakeholders and how you can properly address their concerns, and identify any resistance that needs to be overcome. Positive attitudes need to be promoted and used to influence others.

It is critical to influence *owners* and *managers* positively so that they understand the objectives and benefits of the necessary changes due to the new digital strategy and that they are able to communicate consistently with each other and within their own groups.

Owners—Management team, senior business unit managers, business partners, etc:

- Business benefits of implementing the new digital strategy and a governance framework to run and monitor the programs

- Why we need to do it—Reality check of where we are as an organization and the risks and opportunities we as a company and an industry are facing

- The impact the changes will have on the overall business strategy in the short and long term

- Commitment to support the implementation roadmap and the action plans the project consists of.

Managers — Business, project, program and change managers, users, technical delivery and support teams, key players, e.g. business sponsors, project champions, relationship managers and internal communications teams, contract and procurement management. Peripheral players/influencers/ policy owners, e.g. HR, facilities management and legal teams from contractual to compliance and ethics:

- Business benefits of implementing the new digital strategy and a governance framework to run and monitor the programs

- Why you need to do it—Reality check of where we are as an organization and the risks and opportunities we as a company and an industry are facing

- How does your role and responsibility change and how will it affect you

- You need to change, not as a person but in the way you work—and that is good

- Why we need a performance measurement program to provide independent assessment and assurance and how it will affect you

- Create a clear relation to the projects and to real business risks and benefits that matter to the individuals you are communicating with.

When communicating the need for improved digital programs and governance framework, it is best practice to emphasize the *upside* and the *downside* of controlling risks and maximizing opportunity. The "downside" business risks are financial losses, damage to reputation, loss of service, etc. The "upside" business risks of not exploiting digital programs and big data effectively can be loss of competitive advantage, inefficiencies, failure to respond to changing markets, etc. If upside and downside risks are not communicated effectively, and instead are surrounded by hype and complexity, then stakeholders will not appreciate their real impact, take the issues seriously, or be motivated to insist on better governance. In your communication you must emphasize the negative business impact of misaligned digital strategies, the misuse of technology, badly managed operations, and ineffective project management, and show how these risks can be mitigated by effective controls. Strive to use a common business language even when your team is presenting technological, legal and regulatory risks. In order to best influence stakeholders, and communicate the major objectives and benefits of implementing new or improving existing digital programs and put in place a governance framework throughout the organization, the right language must be used.

A positive and constructive way to communicate risks without coming across as a fear monger is through presenting case studies and results from pilot programs that have impacted your business or other businesses to illustrate how issues may arise.

Use the case studies:

- To identify relevant examples of digital strategy and governance providing real and measurable business benefits

- To illustrate how effective governance has identified risk to the business, its objectives and strategy, and brokered an alternative solution

- To show business benefits as a direct result of effective performance measurement, e.g. innovation, reduced costs, improved quality, productivity, reputation and marketing advantages.

Critical success factors for communicating your new digital strategy and governance framework and to manage change during implementation:

- Involve all relevant stakeholders in a facilitated workshop environment

- Get clear ownership and funding commitment for all planned communications

- Monitor and track your internal communications efforts as you would measure any communications campaign.

Effective and transparent communications will ensure that "everyone is on the same page"—that key issues have been grasped, that objectives have been positively accepted by management and staff, and that everyone understands their role. Every organization will have its own existing culture and should choose their digital governance approach based on what will most likely work best with their culture. The roadmap to follow for cultural change and effective communication will therefore be unique for each organization.

(23) Implementation Planning and Tactical Roadmap

The implementation of digital strategy and governance is a mind-boggling exercise. I have been at this crossroads with companies and felt their frustrations, fears and exhaustion at what they are about to attempt. Staring at the digital ecosystem, stakeholder requirements and KPIs for a corporation can bring about apathy from the most ardent corporate manager. The sense of a lack of resources and capabilities locks in and hasty and poor decisions can get made that eliminate vital parts of the strategy because they get deemed too costly or complicated to implement. I cannot stress enough the use of the portfolio management tool described earlier in this book so you can stack implementation and implement low cost/high benefit solutions first. Because if you reduce the overall budgets for programs to a point where no change is really possible and essentially things will remain as they are and you are stuck with another set of costly "paper strategies."

The key at this crucial intersection is the development of a tactical roadmap that stacks the rollout of your programs into manageable and measurable pilots based on portfolio management framework. The goal of these pilot programs is that they grow based on their success through a test, analyze, optimize and scale approach. Another important reason to recommend the pilot approach is that implementing and activating a corporate digital strategy all at once is simply too much with too high a risk of something going wrong. Great planning is essential, but it does not necessarily make every project a success. For this reason starting small or at a baseline where most critical objectives are met and then scaling your programs based on measurable success factors, greatly reduces risks to your organization.

Pilots can take many forms depending on the system of the program being rolled out. Take a pilot approach the next time you are going to rebuild your website because redesign is needed to meet new design esthetics: the old looks old, you need a better and easier-to-use content management system to implement your content strategy, or a series of new functionalities are needed and the cost of reworking the old code is greater than developing a new site. Regardless, with a pilot approach your website should be launched with only the content and functionalities needed to kick off your content marketing plan and conversion strategies. Then you implement a paid media strategy designed to drive traffic to key areas—first to set a baseline for performance and then to optimize content and conversion paths. Once you have enough traffic and have a sense of your target audience's behavior, scale the site by adding more optimized content and conversion paths.

A social media pilot on Facebook could focus content toward one demographic and the brand programs geared for them. Implement strategies that are geared toward generating likes and valuable information exchanges with your customers. Use paid media strategies to drive traffic to your page and measure against existing brand-specific KPIs. If your analysis reveals positive drivers, make sure your teams involved are comfortable in their roles before the scope is increased and the program scaled.

Since many pilots will fall under different teams in the organization it is possible to launch multiple pilots simultaneously to speed up the total roll out as long as the organization has the resources to do so. It is important however to launch the pilots in the right sequence. I divide pilots into two main groups:

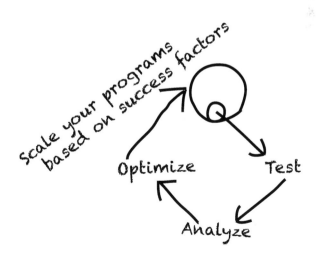

Figure 23.1   TAOS

1. Proof point pilots. Here we are looking for quick and specific answers to help in the decision process and the development of a business case for new or realigned programs.

2. Program launch pilots. These are essentially a scaled and measurable approach to a program rollout.

Each of your pilots must be detailed in your business case with real opportunities for the business identified with practical and useful governance approaches described in understandable processes and language so that all stakeholders can see the benefit of participating in the programs. Then, select champions for your pilots and give them mandates and authority to see them through. Make sure the performance measures applied will clearly articulate the benefits to the organization in the areas they champion. If the programs are successful and can be scaled up, your organization will have identified and made available resources with the skills and capabilities needed to go to the next level. Nothing will kill the motivation of a champion faster than having his or her success limited by bad planning or decision-making. And the last thing you want to do is to kill your champion's motivation, so pay close attention to the implementation planning stage and make sure nothing is overlooked.

These are some additional implementation planning activities that allow everyone to review and take another look at the prepared plans, people, systems and performance measures:

• Identify expert input providers from internal or external resources

- Establish digital governance teams by business function and select members for the cross-organizational governance management team

- Identify digital "hotspots" in the organization, and where governance could enable increased profits and lower risk and where current approaches have not worked or caused serious problems

- Identify the optimal skill sets and capabilities needed from people involved in the different teams

- Identify existing good practice or successes that could be built on or shared across the organization and show how best practice should continuously be shared as programs become up and running

- Identify cost/benefit arguments for each system and business function in order to document why change is needed

- Identify inconsistencies and redundancies in process and practice across business functions

- Identify new opportunities for business units to get involved and benefit from digital systems and the data they generate

- Do some gap analysis against industry best practice and explore opportunities to adopt the industry best practice model or standards framework

- Create a measurement approach for an area or activity to expose actual evidence of problems in order to show your teams the vital importance of an active performance measurement program.

—— 0 ——

As stated, flipping the switch and going live with the complete digital strategy is simply too much for most organizations. Most people that are part of the process have other things on their plates as well. For other business-critical tasks and to counteract the risk of exposing the company to a shortfall of resources and other risk scenarios I recommend the development of a tactical roadmap that stacks the rollout into manageable and measurable pilots, but there are some other critical success factors when rolling out a digital strategy using stacked pilot programs you should pay attention to. An approved business case is a given.

Good project management is paramount and keep in mind that management complexities increase the further into the core team's tasks you get where multiple performance measures are analyzed to aid in the scaling of programs.

Manage digital programs like you manage the rest of the business and set your expectations correctly. Adapt convincing best practice reference programs and first address quick wins to demonstrate results and realize benefits before attempting major changes, using the test, analyze, optimize, and scale approach described above.

PART VI

The Governance

(24) The Governance of Digital Programs and Systems

Digital governance is not just a communications, marketing and IT issue or of interest to them only. In its broadest sense it is a part of the overall governance of an organization, but with a specific focus on improving the results, management and control of digital systems, platforms and communications, and the data they generate for the benefit of all stakeholders. I say all stakeholders since in today's world of total access all involved with a company will interact with its digital systems, benefit from them and become part of the data sets. But, ultimately, digital governance is the responsibility of company leadership and they must ensure that along with other critical business activities digital programs are adequately governed.

In line with this, Accenture defines digital governance to be "the organization, process and performance management model required to facilitate cross-silo decision making on

standards, customer experiences and capability investments across digital channels web, mobile and social."[1]

Digital governance is a relatively new concept as a defined discipline and is still evolving. At its foundation it is simply a good idea—and it is also an imperative. Digital governance is part of the ongoing push to reduce costs, knock down silos and instill a better decision-making process for all digital investments.

Although the principles are not new, actual implementation requires new thinking because of the special nature of many digital programs—they do not live in only one business unit and they are multifaceted. Many of the programs go across the organization and they produce benefits and risks in several areas of a company. Therefore, digital strategy and governance spans the culture, organization, policy and practices that provide for brand and business management and control across five key areas:

- **Alignment**—Provide for strategic direction and the alignment of digital programs and business goals.

- **Value delivery**—Oversee that the organization's digital strategy is designed to get maximum business value from digital programs and systems.

- **Risk management**—Ascertain that processes are in place to ensure that risks are adequately managed and that crises can be handled.

---

1 Digital Governance: Good for Citizens, Good for Government. Accenture 2012.

- **Resource management**—Ensure that there are adequate skill and resource capabilities and an infrastructure to support current and expected future business requirements.

- **Performance measurement**—Verify strategic compliance and achievement of strategic objectives through ongoing measurements of ongoing programs and all campaign activity against set KPIs.

The digital governance of a company's programs, services and systems harbored in its digital strategy is not something achieved by a mandate or setting of rules. It is an ongoing activity that requires a continuous improvement mentality and responsiveness to a fast-changing business environment. It requires a commitment from the top of the organization to instill a better way of dealing with the management and control of what the term digital covers in form of systems, platforms, communications, data, and the people involved.

(25) The Importance of Performance Measurement

In 2012 I was working with a corporate HR organization that was spending millions in recruiting globally. Initially we were going to discuss ways to use social media to get in dialogue with "passive" job seekers. In growing industries with shortage of talent, activating "passive" job seekers, talent employed and not currently looking, is essential to fill open positions. Social media is ideal for this "soft" conversion. In tough labor markets parts of HR's job is that of marketers and sales people and you rarely find those profiles within the human resources field. This is a problem in companies where HR and marketing exist within silos and dialog between the two are rare.

Activating and maturing "passive" job seekers or prospects is very similar to selling complex products or services in business-to-business markets. Your goal is to generate relevant traffic to a place where your prospect will convert to follow your content marketing or knowledge exchange with the goal that they keep your brand at top of mind when they enter the purchase cycle or in this case—job change mode. If your content marketing

strategy is great you might even fast-forward the job change mode. This thinking was foreign to the HR team in question. They provided budgets to marketing which spent the funds like they normally did by creating an advertising campaign to drive traffic to a campaign website where the thought was that the prospect would consume content that would entice them to click on the career site on the corporate website. There the hope was that the "passive" job seeker would become "active" and apply for a job. Needless to say this was a money drain without any results. Clicks from campaign site to main site were virtually non-existent and vital jobs remained vacant. To the marketing teams' defense I will say that they are not lead generators. They are brand marketers.

What we had here were two teams spending money in an area where neither had any expertise, but that is not why I'm telling this story here. This chapter is about performance measurement. The problem was that each business unit involved had their own performance measures and the teams did not share their data. Marketing was concerned with campaign impressions, how many saw their creative work—an important measure for a branding campaign. Next they looked at traffic driven to the campaign site. Job done. The corporate web team looked at the website analytics and generated traffic reports based on that. These reports had no purpose since input to the system and output from the system was not analyzed. HR was counting applications to job interview ratios as a benchmark on their ability to attract relevant prospects. So if marketing was adverting for product development people and a cook for one of their employee cafeterias were hired, each of their measurement systems could rate that as a success. The lack of a holistic performance measurement program was at the heart of their problem.

A tough challenge faced by managers and business leaders trying to manage digital systems, platforms and services and the data they generate in today's turbulent economy and complex technical environment is knowing whether your company is on course and being able to predict and anticipate opportunities and threats before it is too late. Needless to say, it is vital for every part of your digital ecosystem—whether it is a permanent program or a periodic campaign—that data are collected and KPIs are being measured. Besides meeting your digital strategy goals it is crucial that all these measuring points are tied together and track business-critical objectives.

Measuring every part of your digital ecosystem will give you a lot of data and contain multiple data sets, but it does not need to be a complex task for the assigned teams if the process of how to track and measure the KPIs is well defined. Even when you expand a company's performance measurement to include a wider set of publicly available data, such as social media or other text-based data for analysis, the complexity of the process will still be manageable if the groundwork is done and the foundation set. So it is important that you evaluate the scope of analysis needed for your company based on what is really needed to best meet business goals, and then set the frequency of reports based on their risk, opportunity and business value.

Your performance measures should address two aspects:

- **Outcome focused**—are your digital strategies meeting your objectives?

- **Process focused**—are your processes operating effectively and likely to lead to objectives being met?

The measuring of digital performance is just as necessary and should be just as transparent and reliable as the measurement and reporting of financial results is to corporate governance. Although it is not guided and enforced through SOX-type legislation, the mindset you apply to the task should be in the same vein. If you are able to communicate and transplant that mentality to your performance measurement program you are well on the road to succeed. Performance management is important because it verifies the achievement of strategic objectives and provides a review of performance and the contribution of the digital ecosystem to the business. The contributions by each of your digital programs may be seen through the analysis of data against set KPIs. Some KPIs will track actual return on investment (ROI) where that is feasible, such as campaigns, lead generation, content programs, etc. Other KPIs will be tracked based on a wider set of values. A website for instance will serve a broad set of business units and will contain both ROI-based KPIs in regards to lead generation and broader value-based KPIs such as brand sentiment score.

A practical and effective way to analyze data, big or otherwise, is an essential part of any digital governance program. An example: a KPI for your media relation team is to promote your company's point of view on a challenging industry issue. As part of their process they use several digital tools such as email, twitter and the media relations section on the website to address journalists and related stakeholders. To reach industry experts, internal stakeholders and your industry's professional community they use a blog and LinkedIn. In addition they have a content and engagement strategy on Facebook targeting the general public and non-governmental organizations (NGOs). If your measurement program in such cases only looked at analytics and counted articles placed, you would only get part of the story, but if you combined that with a text analysis using data collected from the internet to analyze the spread of related information and the general sentiment regarding the relevant topics you will get a much better reading of their performance. You can set up similar scenarios for your product innovation teams. Performance measurement is important in setting the course for product development. By looking at multiple data sets such as customer service correspondence, website traffic, online text analysis, etc. you can get a better view of what your customers think and what they want.

Providing a transparent assessment of your employees and suppliers capabilities is also an integral part of performance measurement. Here it can be used to provide an early warning system for risks and pitfalls that might otherwise have been missed, including cost over-runs or budget short falls. Too few companies apply a pilot approach to their digital programs and scale them through tests and analyses, thus wasting buckets of money on projects and campaigns that will never show any ROI. Performance measurement provides transparency of digital related costs. This is increasingly important since it is a growing post in many organizations' operating expenses. But performance measurement reporting is not just to get advance warnings when things may be going wrong, it is a key method to identify success factors and optimize them through your programs.

For performance measurement to be successful, it is important to understand who your stakeholders are and what their specific requirements and drivers are so that the performance measurements will be meaningful to them. A performance measurement—similar to any big data analysis program—is only effective if it serves to communicate to all who need to know what is important and then motivates them and sets guidelines for constructive actions and alignments to common business objectives. The measurement reporting is not an end in itself but a means to take constructive action and to learn from real experience through your digital programs. Concise and understandable communication and clear accountability are therefore critical success factors if findings are to be turned into effective action to improve your business landscape and your position in it.

Defining the KPIs for your performance measurement program and identifying which data sets to analyze for the different KPIs is a key component of digital governance. Performance measurement done right verifies the achievement of strategic business objectives and provides for a review of the contribution of digital systems, platforms and services through:

- **Alignment**—monitoring the strategic direction of and the alignment of digital programs and the business

- **Value Delivery**—assessing whether the digital ecosystem is providing optimal business value and assessing ROI

- **Risk Management**—monitoring whether risks are being identified and managed and measuring the cost and benefit of risk management investments including brand reputation

- **Resource Management**—measuring the effectiveness of sourcing and the use of resources across the organization, the aggregate funding of digital programs at the enterprise level, and measuring digital capability and infrastructure compared to current and expected future business requirements.

Performance measurement is a framework and toolset to help drive your business. To that end, make sure you have performance measures in place to ensure that the outcomes of digital activities are aligned with your company's immediate and future goals. Moreover, internal process measures are required to ensure that the employees have the right processes and tools for delivering the intended outcomes of the digital strategy on-time and cost-effectively. Advanced performance measurement enables the measurement of key aspects of digital capability such as creativity and agility, the development of new solutions, the ability to operate reliable and secure services in an increasingly demanding environment, and the development of human resources and skills. The introduction of a performance measurement system focused on a few key strategic objectives can be an excellent way to kick-start a digital governance initiative, providing, perhaps for the first time, transparency of critical activities and a way to bridge the communication gap between owners of digital initiatives and corporate stakeholders.

Analyzing the data generated from your digital programs quantifies how well digital activities are doing towards achieving their designated goals. Adding additional sources of information to your performance measures, including such things as content quality and resource training, will inform stakeholders how their digital strategy is performing against business objectives. A performance measurement report should communicate what is important for the business. A consistent view of the data over time will enable your teams to work toward optimizing your digital strategy, achieve your business goals, and improve your organization.

A performance measurement program based on an analysis of all the data from your digital ecosystem should help you to grow the company through sales and improved products and product mix by focusing on the customer to increase satisfaction. Growth could also come from improving processes so that problems are anticipated and prevented and by better understanding of costs and therefore reducing program expenditures.

To achieve this your performance measurement program must be defined in a common language appropriate and understandable for the audience, and approved by your stakeholders. The program must be in keeping with the culture and style of the organization and include both positive measures to motivate and negative measures that lead to process improvements. Your performance measures must be derived from business objectives both objective and subjective and be flexible and responsive to changing priorities and requirements. To enable hierarchical reporting your reports should be consolidated and easy to read and support benchmarking internally between peer groups and externally with best practice. And finally your digital performance measures should be integrated if possible with any existing business level performance measurement system.

To support digital governance the following top fifteen areas to measure are recommended:

1. Business, marketing and communications goals alignment

2. Major project delivery performance (objectives, time and budget)

3. Overall financial performance (costs v. budgets)

4. ROI for digital investments (business benefit)

5. Status of reputation and critical risks

6. Performance with respect to reliability and availability of critical services

7. Complaints and customer perception

8. Number of significant reactive fixes to errors

9. SLA performance by third parties

10. Relationships with suppliers (quality and value)

11. Capability e.g. process maturity

12. HR measures for people involved in digital activities

13. Internal and external benchmarks

14. Meeting stakeholder objectives

15. Business continuity status.

Finally, here are five you should avoid:

1. Too much focus on technical measures (especially if they are not aligned with strategic objectives)

2. Lack of ownership and accountability

3. Measures that are not straightforward to interpret or encourage counter-productive behavior

4. Measures that are expensive to collect or not focused on priority areas

5. Too many measures obscuring relevant and important information.

Effective performance measurement through strategically selected datasets will enable management and other stakeholders to know whether or not the organization is meeting its current and planned objectives. It provides a transparent and objective communication mechanism, as long as the measures are understandable and agreed upon by everyone involved.

(26) Training, Guidelines, Responsibility Structure, Content Calendars, Accounts Info and Password Storage

The benefits from digital strategy implementation can come from the most unexpected places. A year ago I was working with a large retail operation to implement a series of pilot programs with the purpose to learn the effect different activities in social media could have on different aspects of their business. The pilots were structured to generate enough data and real-world experience to inform future strategies and optimize planned

programs before a larger and broader rollout across several countries. One of our pilots was testing the business impact of handling customer service "calls" on Facebook. Some of our performance measurements were identical to current KPIs: Positive, neutral or negative resolution, time to resolution, and number of interactions to resolution. Then we had some pilot-specific measurements such as to see if opening our doors on Facebook would reduce over-all call-center loads or if the resources spent on social media came in addition to existing costs. In addition we were tracking more general things such as brand sentiment. The customer service teams in two countries were part of this pilot.

Naturally the teams had been trained in dealing with customers on the phone, but we discovered that no training had been provided for writing even though email had a solid percentage of customer service inquiries. Since Facebook provided a platform where a customer service issue would be shared openly, and not one-on-one as in an email exchange, we decided that training in writing short and concise messages would be essential for the execution of a valid pilot test.

What we found after a four months pilot was that the training in writing had improved the overall performance of the teams involved and not just their performance on Facebook. Fewer interactions were needed to come to a satisfactory resolution in all channels. The result was that the company now has implemented training in writing as a standard process for all customer service units. This is to illustrate how important and beneficial training programs are to an organization. Employees feel the company is investing in them and helping them through corporate and technological change instead of replacing them. In return the company gets better performing people.

In this chapter I will give some pointers for training, guidelines, responsibility structure, content calendars, accounts information, and password storage. These topics do not have much in common except that they are very tactical and always come up when digital governance is discussed.

TRAINING

Training, as the story above shows, is important to an organization and can demonstrate its benefits in many forms. When it comes to digital governance we can divide training into three areas: systems, skills and behavior.

The training in how to operate and manage a system such as a content management system (CMS), customer relationship management program (CRM), ecommerce platform, etc. must have continuity and the actual training and training materials are often supplied by the vendor and the responsibility of the vendor that supplied the software. The key here is redundancy and continuity. You do not want the absence of one or two people to prohibit a program to respond to a request. The same is the case if a person leaves the company.

Skills training, as in the story above, can be about learning to write in a certain format or for a specific purpose, but it can also include more complex tasks such as reading and understanding online analytics in the context of a business and its performance measurement program.

Behavioral training is most often in relation to social media and how to conduct oneself and respond in the different media. This can be a HR recruitment team using LinkedIn to take direct contact with prospects, executives getting

coaching in how to represent the company in front of the camera for online videos, or a corporate social responsibility (CSR) representative dealing with the criticisms from an NGO.

A few weeks back we were shooting videos of a CEO and the chief architect from a software company for an upcoming product launch. I met with the CEO in advance of the video shoot to discuss his approach and his sales and positioning angle for his two-minute video. We have a great working relationship and it did not take us long to come up with a good approach. As the meeting concluded I asked if he would need assistance with the script or some front-of-camera training. He smilingly dismissed my suggestions. This was material he presented daily and often in front of large audiences or with the pressure of closing a deal. The day came and he became out-of-character nervous as the shoot approached, but reassured the team that it would be no problem. When he received the rough edit of his video he was not happy with his performance. It didn't look good. We decided to shoot it again with training this time. He later told me that he had thought it would be easy and now had a different kind of respect for those who work in front of the camera and make it seem easy and natural.

GUIDELINES

Guidelines, as opposed to instructions, describe a suggested best practice of doing something. In regards to digital strategy two of the most common guidelines are on general online behavior and how to respond to online posts by customers or other stakeholders. I have included a sample of both below.

Sample generic social media guideline:

We are guided by the values—open, caring, courageous and hands-on—that we live by as a company and as employees of this company.

This is our social media policy. It is intended to outline how these values should be demonstrated in the social media space. It will guide your participation in this arena when you are speaking about the company as a private person, as well as when you act on behalf of COMPANY.

Transparency every time we engage in social media. If you speak on behalf of COMPANY you must make sure to state explicitly who you are and what your affiliation is with the company. Only speak on behalf of us if you are authorized to do so.

As a private person, if you engage in a discussion that relates to COMPANY you must explicitly state that you are speaking on behalf of yourself and not the company.

Protect our stakeholders' and our colleagues' privacy. Be conscientious and caring when you express opinions, post material or take part in debates.

Respect copyrights, trademarks and other third-party rights when you re-submit, share or post information and material in general in the social media space. Respect the individual's privacy and make sure that you have acceptance if, for example, you post images of your colleagues in the social media space. Don't share any company-sensitive information and remember that you may be personally liable for copyright infringement.

Be responsible in your use of links. Do not knowingly use, promote or affiliate yourself or COMPANY with websites or applications that use excessive tracking software, adware, malware or spyware.

Be vigilant. Before opening shared files or following links to other pages, assess whether the material looks suspicious.

Best practice. Listen to the community that is participating in the social forum and be compliant with the relevant local, national or international guidelines and regulations. Remain calm, behave with respect and act with a hands-on approach.

Be professional. Be constructive and act within the law. Be calm, show respect and demonstrate responsibility. Strive for simplicity and clarity and remain loyal. Be truthful, precise and ethical.

The Internet remembers. Be sure to say what you mean and mean what you say. Be aware that what you say is permanent and that, sometimes, silence is golden. Search engines and affiliated technologies make it virtually impossible to take something back.

In short, use common sense when using social media. Always keep our policies and values in mind, as social media are just another platform for our communication.

User post-response guideline.

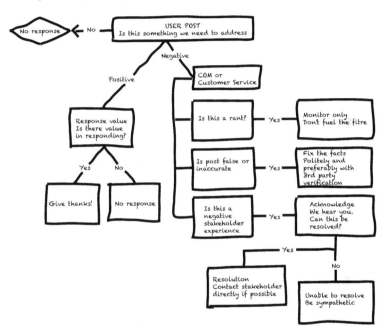

Figure 26.1   Response guideline

RESPONSIBILITY STRUCTURE

To determine who does what and divide and organize the responsibilities of your digital ecosystem by channel or platform is as crucial as it is helpful for the people involved and for the safe continuation of programs. It is great to have a simple overview of who owns what and who should be doing what in form of a diagram as depicted below. For more complex tasks, written descriptions of jobs and responsibilities may also be needed.

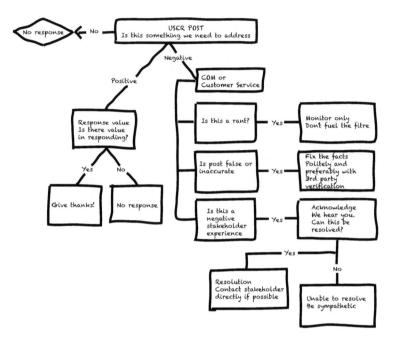

Figure 26.2   Responsibility diagram

EDITORIAL CALENDAR

The purpose of an editorial calendar for a company is to have a visual representation or view of your content schedule. This helps a company to plan resources and keep their publishing platforms fresh and interesting for stakeholders. An editorial calendar is not a management tool for daily updates and quick responses to issues. To make your content calendar that advanced will just complicate the project management of the schedule.

The complexities of your content marketing strategy and the number of platforms on which your company publishes content will drive the format of the calendar or the system you build it on. Excel is a great tool to build a tailored calendar suited to your needs, but if you have a need for multi-office collaboration you may look for a more specialized off-the-shelf online solution you can use as is or with some customization.

For large multi-national companies one calendar could become too complex and work against its purpose. For companies where factors such as culture and socio economic and demographic realities determine product mix, language, and the priority of content topics, a multi-calendar solution would work best. Set up regular meetings to share ideas and sync plans for international projects. Advertising campaigns and other campaign-related content production should always live on stand-alone calendars since the same teams will rarely be managing campaigns and ongoing editorial content unless you are a start-up or a small to medium business where a few people wear multiple hats.

ACCOUNTS INFORMATION AND PASSWORDS

There is a surprising number of companies, large and small, that I have worked with, that have not had a system for storing and organizing accounts information and passwords. Information such as where things are hosted, where the code is located, who worked on it last, user names and passwords, analytics software, original content, rights documents to photos and videos, etc. must be stored and managed properly. You should have a company-wide policy for this.

Not much more to say on this except to get it in order and keep it that way. This is important for everyone's peace of mind.

㉗ Ongoing Communications Strategy

Critical to the success of any digital strategy and governance initiative is an effective communications plan. The communications plan should be based on a well-defined influencing strategy. That may sound menacing, but behaviors may need to be changed and care should therefore be taken to ensure that participants will be motivated and can see the benefits of the new approaches, as well as understand the consequences of accepting responsibility. If this is not positively communicated, then digital governance will not be perceived as part of the corporate mission with C-level support. Management will resist it as a barrier to getting the job done, a deviation from current priorities, or another fad.

Every organization will have its own existing culture and choice of digital governance paradigm that it wishes to adopt. The roadmap to follow for cultural change and effective communication will therefore be unique for your specific situation. So to set up a working roadmap you must analyze the existing state and define the desired state of your digital governance. A good way to get started is to gather your team with members from all business units involved and write

down two lists under the headlines "Current state" and
"Desired state."

It may end up looking something like this:

Figure 27.1 State of business

The communication strategy you choose to implement
should identify opportunities for the active involvement of
stakeholders in developing the governance approach, planning
and implementing process management changes, and ideally
building specific change objectives/targets into personal
performance plans. The stakeholders are likely themselves to
be the targets of change and should be involved in discussing/
evolving responses to the change via collaborative workshops,
focus groups etc.

The influencing strategies need to be designed to work in
specific situations with the individual influence targets
identified:

• Focus on roles and responsibilities

- Identify an overall sponsor and steering group with specific tasks and responsibilities for leading the change

- Ensure there is a complete structure of cascaded sponsorship down to team/line manager level.

Focus on individual situations

- Identify champions (those high on interest and/or influence)

- Use successes as benchmarks.

Disseminate across teams and support formation of new teams.

28 System and Reputational Risk Management

The management of risks is a cornerstone of digital governance, ensuring that the strategic objectives of the business are not jeopardized. Risks related to digital programs are increasingly a leadership issue as the impact on the business of a failed or mismanaged project or a thunderous flow of negative posts in social media, can have devastating consequences. However, managing risks and exercising proper governance is a challenging experience for business managers faced with an overwhelming amount of data, communication-channel proliferation, technical complexity, a dependence on an increasing number of service providers, and limited reliable risk monitoring information. As a consequence, management is often concerned whether risks are being cost effectively addressed, and they need assurance that risks are under control.

You must be conscious and promote within the organization the view that risk taking is an essential element of business

today. Success will come to those organizations that identify and manage risks most effectively. Risk is as much about failing to grasp an opportunity as it is about doing something badly or incorrectly. There has been a prolific fear among company leaderships to actively enter into the social realm for fear that it will trigger negative reputational consequences—as if staying out would limit negative comments. The protectionist thought of "don't stir the fire" remains. The fear of doing something badly can materialize in year-long committee work bogging down the development of new systems and making them obsolete by the time the programs are launched. Risk is essential to success.

The universal need to demonstrate good enterprise governance to corporate stakeholders and business leadership is a driver for increased risk and reputation management activities in large organizations. Part of this is ascertaining that there is transparency about the significant risks the enterprise is facing and clarifying the risk-taking or risk-avoidance policies of the enterprise. The leadership must do this since the final responsibility for risk management rests with them. When delegating to executive management, they should make sure the constraints of that delegation are communicated and clearly understood. In addition, leadership should insist that risk management is embedded in the operation of the enterprise, so it can respond quickly to changing risks and report immediately to appropriate levels of management, supported by agreed upon principles of escalation (what to report, when, where and how). The benefits are that a transparent and proactive risk management approach can create a competitive advantage that can be exploited, and that the system of internal control put in place to manage risks has the capacity to generate cost-efficiency.

—— 0 ——

Good communication is as important to risk management as to all other aspects of governance. To enable effective governance, risks related to digital programs should always be expressed in a business context rather than in the technical language favored by many IT departments or as the loosely defined reputational risks defined by advertising centric marketing and social media teams. The following generic structure for expressing risks in any organization is suggested:

- Business specific risks (e.g. operational risk of orders not being received through the ecommerce portal)

- Reputation specific risks (e.g. reputation attacks in social media)

- Generic common system risks (e.g. system availability risks)

- Specific system risks (e.g. denial of service attack on customer ordering system).

Business risks are affected by the management style, culture, risk appetite, national and international regulations, and industry sector factors such as competition, reputation etc. Digital program risks can be similarly affected. There is no single accepted set of generic digital risk definitions, but these headings can be used as a guide:[1]

- Investment or expense risk

- Access or security risk

---

1 Taken from a global study by the Economist Intelligence Unit in 2002.

- Integrity risk

- Relevance risk

- Availability risk

- Infrastructure risk

- Project ownership risk

- Missed opportunity.

Add reputational risk to that list and you will have a starting point to build your risk program.

(29) How to Obtain, Develop, Retain and Verify Competence

Good people or the right people in the right positions are a key to the success of digital strategy implementation and ongoing governance of digital programs. When considering who to place in digital governance lead positions, especially when creating an initial project team, staffing from the inside could be a great way to go if you have the right size organization. People in a number of existing positions may be excellent candidates. The following people can be effective in digital governance roles:

- Project managers

- Risk managers

- Marketing and communications managers

- Business analysts

- Infrastructure management

- Procurement and contract management

- Quality control and assurance management

- Business relationship management

- IT and marketing program managers

- Designers and copywriters.

As you can see from this list there is a need for breadth of business, marketing and IT knowledge rather than too narrow a specialization. For smaller organizations or where resources are already strapped for time, developing the skills needed is another good option. Regardless, companies need a skills development plan in place for all those involved in the digital strategy execution, performance measurement and governance.

Demonstrating commitment by senior management to the importance of digital governance and the value of being competent, removing cultural barriers, and improving communications are critical success factors for improving competence.

The most effective way to develop and retain skills to run and manage digital programs and their governance is by establishing standards and practices within the organization rather than only within individuals. This reduces reliance on key individuals and ensures that sustainable processes are put into place. Below are some techniques for improving and retaining skills within your company:

- Obtain external experience to help position and challenge internal activities. Adopt "360 degree feedback" or other holistic performance feedback methodologies

- Consider appointing executive-mentoring advisors to bring management up to speed on the understanding and use of digital programs and systems

- Consider external executive digital awareness courses

- Foster cultural change activities

- Enable job exchanges to improve awareness

- When training, focus on specialized and relevant areas and use interactive formats that encourage engagement and dialog

- Organize internal events to raise awareness

- Rotate involvement in governance meetings to improve understanding

- Use the results of assessments and maturity modeling to raise awareness of governance issues, gaps in capability, and impact on the business of program weaknesses

- Ensure that the management and control of digital is taken seriously

- Manage the transfer of skills from the specialists to the organization. Skills development is often more about learning on the job than about training courses

- Run fire drills and crisis scenarios to test the organization's alertness and ability to deal with high risk situations

- Understand the business, how digital programs affect the business, the digital-related business risks, and why digital needs to be controlled under governance

- Focus on professional training in digital governance and consider certification in relevant skills

- Maintain continuing professional development

- Consider "soft" skills training to improve communication and influencing skills.

At all levels there will be a need to refresh skills continually because of the changing nature of digital, so make sure that all programs are ongoing. Vendors, suppliers and service partners must be valued for their digital skills and encouraged to invest in them. This is especially true of external service providers. Induction training should be required of new joiners, especially those holding key positions in relation to digital programs and systems.

(30) Building Better Partnerships

Every organization relies on numerous partners to support their business and digital strategy. Increasingly the trend is to outsource significant parts of digital programs and critical business processes. It is not unusual for external organizations to provide critical infrastructure services such as software development, maintenance and hosted data centers, and handling direct stakeholder communications as social media managers or content providers in key areas such as investor and media relations.

An effective governance of suppliers is therefore a key component of digital governance, making sure that risks are managed and value is delivered from the investment in supplier products and services. Most organizations are highly dependent on a limited number of key suppliers, often on multi-year contracts; therefore governance should be focused on those relationships with the greatest risk and investment. For supplier governance to be effective the role of the buyer or project owner is crucial. The buyer or project owner should take ownership of the whole transaction from defining requirements and selection all the way through to engagement, operation and termination.

Even when the bulk of digital programs is outsourced, several key functions should be retained in-house because they supply continuity for project owners and other internal stakeholders, provide for the oversight of the outsourcer, are highly specific to the way the business operates, and are strategic for the organization. To some extent, the mix will vary with your reasons for outsourcing and which functions have been outsourced. However, all organizations will need to retain some expertise in strategic functions, such as project oversight, architecture, design, content creation, planning, vendor management, performance measurement, and security.

One of the best ways to establish effective supplier governance is to focus on the relationship. In other words, to define the category of relationship the different vendors or programs fall under. On the one side you have the "commodity" relationship where cost, scalability, response time, geo-location and other hard values can easily determine which vendor to use or measure the success of a relationship. On the other side of the spectrum you find the "value"-based relationship. These are harder to measure because they can contain such "soft" qualities as creativity, industry expertise, know-how, etc. If you look upon this as a line with these two definitions at opposite ends you will be able to place most relationships somewhere on this scale, and this can be a useful tool for the internal team to help choose the right partner or set performance measurement criteria.

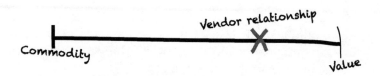

Figure 30.1   Vendor relationship

Sharing this definition and how the team came to it will determine how both parties engage with each other. Commitment by both parties at a senior level to the same definition of the relationship and its performance criteria will increase the responsibility and accountability of senior decision makers on both sides. Specify the definition, performance measurement criteria and governance responsibilities in a "governance schedule" within the contract.

Always try to create a win/win partnership so that both parties are motivated for success—beating down the supplier is generally seen as poor practice, while cooperation and considered openness and mutuality of benefit defines the basis for better working relationships. Your supplier is of course also a stakeholder and will want to ensure that the relationship is properly managed, and that the financial and operational requirements are acceptable. It will be in your interest as the buyer or in your program owner's interest to balance the supplier's needs with your own in order to arrive at a solution that provides reasonable incentives for your supplier while properly meeting your company's needs. Underpinning the supplier relationship there should be formal service-level agreements that define objectives and measures in company relevant terms and are managed according to service management best practices.

Since companies are highly dependent on a limited number of key suppliers, the outsourcing of a function or service is likely to be a major strategic decision, which should be governed carefully. Outsourcing is also a huge global commercial business opportunity for the service providers who will compete fiercely for market shares. In such a complex technical and commercial situation, proper governance is crucial to help avoid potential service failures and large financial losses.

Common causes of outsourcing failures are unclear buyer expectations, misaligned interests, poor governance, poor communication, provider's poor performance, poor cultural fit or that a company's multi-buyer environment has created confusion as to orders and responsibilities.

If the vendor relationship is critical in support of the company's business strategy, which will be the case if significant outsourcing is planned or if critical infrastructure needs to be supported, then your role in ensuring effective governance will be particularly important and should address:

- Independence from the supplier

- Accountability and responsibility for key decisions

- Increasing stakeholder value (both internal and for the supplier)

- Key governance steps at each stage, best defined in a governance schedule in the contract, and in a shared procedure manual where key responsibilities and escalation procedures are defined.

Make sure that the person or team assigned the management responsibility for key supplier partnerships has the right capability to manage the program and provide proper oversight. Your digital ecosystem will present such varied areas of supplier partnerships that you will not find all the right skillsets within one business unit to manage everything from software development to programmatic advertising buying. These managers must also be able to focus on what is critical for the success of the project and ensure that there are clear roles and responsibilities on the customer's side of the relationship. Your supplier manager should have the support from an executive level sponsor who is responsible and accountable for all significant decisions regarding key suppliers. The goal is to create a long-term mutually-beneficial relationship.

If you are managing system development programs, ensure conformance where necessary and compatibility with in-house technical standards and all relevant legal and regulatory requirements. It is important that there is someone in-house with at least some technical understanding of the project so the organization does not become overly dependent on a supplier and that the risks have been evaluated if proprietary technologies are used.

Here are some tips:

- Standardize solutions wherever possible

- Set realistic expectations regarding service delivery

- Take time to understand product and service offerings

- Ensure that there is good control of the internal environment affected by the external supplier

- Take care to manage all staff-related issues

- Make sure there is a process for both parties to follow

- Build into the requirements and contract plans for transition/transformation from the current state to an outsourced service

- Approach contracts and relationships in a balanced way, ensuring that risks have been considered in the context of the value expected from the supplier

- Avoid the danger of mixed messages coming from different parts of your organization

- Make sure that there is top-down management commitment to support all key decisions.

To monitor and measure a technical vendor relationship, identify a limited range of meaningful and measurable key measures and take ownership and define and obtain agreement for all measures such as performance, financial, risks, compliance, relationship, value added, and delivery.

The following steps are suggested to select a supplier:

1. Research the market to identify preferred suppliers

2. Consider the size of supplier compared to your organization and your requirements

3. Consider the need to integrate several suppliers

4. Do due diligence reviews

5. Prepare an effective RFP

6. Meet with key people within the suppliers organization

7. Consider pilots and pre-project trials

8. Check track record

9. Consider impact of any off-shore situations.

To re-cap, one of the best ways to establish effective supplier governance is to focus on and define the relationship and how both parties engage with each other. There must be commitment by both parties at a senior level and responsibility and accountability by senior decision makers on both sides that also make sure that each party understands their role.

(31) Legal and Regulatory Aspects of Digital Governance

Like Facebook and Google, Netflix recently settled a class-action privacy lawsuit by agreeing to donate millions of dollars to nonprofits. And, as with Facebook and Google, not everyone is happy about the agreement.

Some Netflix users are so unhappy that they're asking the 9th Circuit Court of Appeals to vacate the deal, arguing that it doesn't benefit the people who were affected by the potential privacy glitch.

The lawsuit centered on allegations that Netflix violated a 1988 video privacy law by holding on to subscribers' records after they had canceled their memberships. That law, which was passed after a newspaper obtained the video rental records of

Supreme Court nominee Robert Bork, prohibits movie rental services from disclosing consumers' records without their consent. It also requires services to delete users' personal information as soon as possible.

The Netflix settlement requires the company to stop linking former subscribers' names with their movie-viewing history, and to pay $6.5 million to 20 nonprofits and up to $2.25 million to the lawyers who sued on behalf of consumers. But it doesn't require Netflix to pay anything to the users whose information was retained.

Wednesday, Oct. 30, 2013
(Source: Media Post Online)

There is a wide range of laws and regulations, some specific to industry sectors, that can have an impact on digital practices, and non-compliance can have serious implications for your business as you can see above. If you are running an ecommerce business with operations in Europe, the United States and South Korea the laws and regulations regarding taxation, privacy and credit card handling will vary greatly, to name a few areas of concern. In addition, there are compliance and ethical issues with legal implication in everything from warehouse employees to vendor relationships. Therefore, every organization must identify the specific regulations affecting them and respond accordingly, and ensure that the roles and responsibilities for understanding legal and regulatory matters are properly defined for each group of internal stakeholders so that each group can apply its specific expertise effectively. External advice must be sought whenever the issues are sufficiently risky or complex.

Every organization relies on a growing number of third parties for the support of digital practices. From a legal and regulatory perspective this means that there is potentially a complex hierarchy of responsibilities that combine to meet the legal and regulatory needs of the company. Ultimately, it is the company's responsibility to ensure that all the right controls are in place with any third party that is relied upon for legal and regulatory compliance.

The impact of not taking sufficient care of legal or regulatory requirements can be considerable, such as loss of reputation, inability to trade, financial penalties and losses, loss of competitive advantage, and loss of opportunity. On the other hand, the benefit of complying with regulatory requirements and using legal measures to protect commercial interests can be considerable. General improvement in overall control of digital programs and systems can reduce losses and administrative costs, lead to a more efficient and effective negotiation of commercial transactions, and strengthen your ability and confidence to take risks—because everyone involved, including management, feels more in control of the programs and systems.

The recent increase in the number of regulations affecting the use of digital systems and programs is due to a number of factors. A greater interest by regulators in the operations of all organizations caused by major corporate financial failures and scandals, are resulting in regulations like the US Sarbanes-Oxley Act forcing Boards of Directors to express opinions about their systems of control. There are also strong concerns for security and privacy fueled by the overall increase in the use of smartphones and networks and the impact of the Internet, and every country has laws to protect personal information and its potential misuse in electronic form.

There is also a growth in the use of computer systems and networks for criminal activity and terrorism, including viruses, hacking, money laundering, and pornography. Add this to the growth in all forms of electronic media and the potential for misuse of valuable information assets, resulting in copyright and intellectual property issues of concern for both vendors and users. In the news as I'm writing this is the hacking of Adobe Systems' data where the estimate is that 89 million private records have been stolen along with some of the company's intellectual property. Globally publicized issues like this are bound to increase demand from the public and political decisions to further increase security demands on digital systems.

The Snowden information leaks and the ongoing debate regarding NSA's spying practices through digital channels will also have an after effect and impact on laws and regulations, and one thing is for certain—it will never become easier or less expensive to comply, and the repercussions for not complying will also get increasingly severe. So expect to see further complexities in regards to your controlled systems and contractual relationships for digital services and products, including outsourcing, managed services, product licenses, intellectual property rights etc.

What may appear to be an initial regulatory burden can become an opportunity to transform to better managed practices if the rules are used positively and applied productively. Compliance with digital-related legal and regulatory requirements and the effective use of legal contracts are clearly part of the effective control and oversight of digital activities by senior management and are therefore key aspects of digital governance. There is a wide range of laws and regulations, some specific to industry sectors, which can have an impact on digital practices. Every organization must identify the specific regulations affecting them and respond accordingly.

The following areas ought to be considered:

- Personal data and privacy

- Corporate governance, financial reporting, stock market requirements

- Money laundering and other criminal acts

- Intellectual property, trademarks and copyright

- Electronic communication, signatures etc.

- Electronic commerce

- Email monitoring, appropriate use and confidentiality

- Social media defamation

- Document and record retention

- Digital-related products and service contracts

- Sector specific regulations e.g. financial, health, pharmaceutical etc.

The following tips will enable an effective ongoing legal and regulatory compliance program and the proper control of legal contracts:

- Establish the right culture to encourage diligence and good controls

- Communication throughout the organization based on leadership mandate is essential to make sure everyone takes the issues seriously and uniformly

- Involve the right people as advisors but do not abdicate responsibility

- Retain responsibility for control and compliance when using service providers

- Standardization and a common approach is the most effective and efficient way to meet compliance requirements

- Integrate compliance objectives into the digital strategy

- Set the tone at the top and ensure that management are actively involved—not just performing a sign-off at the end

- Institutionalize compliance behavior by engaging the governance and risk management groups, those who own the systems and programs, as soon as possible, providing a positive spin. Good controls can be very beneficial, and make compliance normal business practice rather than a project

- To make compliance meaningful and relevant, translate into normal language, explain the business context and carry out awareness training

- Establish mechanisms for evidence and documentation

- Establish metrics for monitoring performance

- Create incentives and/or penalties as part of personal objectives

- Do regular compliance checking and tests

- Do regular reviews of risks (include 3rd parties)

- Have good incident management procedures to learn from legal and regulatory incidents.

Dealing with legal and regulatory requirements and knowing how best to use legal contracts can be challenging for digital practice leaders who are not knowledgeable about legal matters, and for business managers who may not appreciate all the legal risks and issues associated with the use of technology and digital communication. Organizations should therefore ensure that the roles and responsibilities for understanding legal and regulatory matters are properly defined for each group of stakeholders so that each group can apply its specific expertise effectively. External advice must be sought whenever the issues are sufficiently risky or complex.

Conclusion

THINK FAST, BE AGILE, BE READY—YOU'RE ALWAYS ON

With big data emerging as a standard framework for decision making, digital strategy and governance have taken on an increased importance. Marketing and sales have been among the early adaptors that have found return on their big data investment. A clear driver is the rapid growth of programmatic marketing campaigns. Programmatic campaigns are dynamically triggered by predetermined events and ads are deployed according to a set of rules applied by software and algorithms. For a modern marketing organization the leap from programmatic to big data in not hard to justify after you have experienced the increased return from your online campaigns. Often the leap means that unstructured data (i.e. social media text mining) is added to your structured data (i.e. online analytics and ad platform metrics). This enables you to analyze the differences between behavioral patterns and what your customers and targets are actually saying, and this gives you a much better planning environment.

A holistic digital strategy will set you up to take advantage of these trends, and governance is the framework you use to optimize your digital programs and reduce overall risks from the systems. My goal is that this book will provide you with an understanding of what it will take to develop, implement and run a digital strategy. It is not meant as a rigid process document you must follow. Companies have different needs and live in vastly different environments. The internal structure of your organization and the market in which you compete is not going to adapt to your digital strategy process, you must find a process and methodology that works for you. But there are four things you must keep in mind:

- **Think fast**—the pace of digital development does not give you the environment and the luxury of time. I do not promote hasty decisions made without all available information, but if something is not functioning optimally you could lose money and customers if you do not correct it, and the faster you can do it the better. Your teams must be composed in a way and mandates given to promote a decentralized decision environment supported by a culture that accepts and is willing to take risks.

- **Be agile**—Even with the best planning, and even if pilots have been deployed to stake the course it could turn out to be the wrong tactic. Stop it and try something else. If the last 20 years have told us anything it is that the digital landscape changes and the pace of change is constantly speeding up. Don't wait for the market to change. Change the market. Be the disruptor instead of being disrupted.

- **Be ready**—If you are set up for quick decision-making and your organization is agile and able to change, then you really just need to be ready for two main things— opportunity and risk. If opportunity knocks, scale it quickly and if your reputation is under attack in social media, mobilize. Positive and negative crisis preparedness is vital.

- **Always on**—It is a given in today's online marketplace that you are perceived as being always on. Make sure your governance of both your systems and platforms keeps it that way.

Bibliography

Bullish on digital, 2013, McKinsey Global Survey results

The CMO Survey, 2013, The CMOsurvey.org

Dealing with disruption, 16th Annual Global CEO Survey, 2013, PWC

The Digital Advantage: How digital leaders outperform their peers in every industry, 2013, MIT Center for Digital Business and Capgemini Consulting

Digital Governance: Good for Citizens, Good for Government, 2012, Accenture Federal Services

Digital Transformation: A Roadmap For Billion-Dollar Organizations, 2011, MIT Center for Digital Business and Capgemini Consulting

IT Governance, Developing a successful governance strategy, 2005 National Computing Centre

The New Digital Economy, How it will transform business, 2011, Oxford Economics

There are numerous other articles and news stories that have helped shape my view on digital brand strategy. I consume these as my daily routine to keep myself updated. Some articles are found by following certain hash-tags on Twitter, but my regular sources include: *eMarketer, Media Post, Ad Week, Ad Age, Mashable, TechCrunch, Mercury News, Forbes, Wall Street Journal, Economist, Business Insider*, Wikipedia, and many more.

Index

Sales process, 154, 159
Search engines, 21, 70
Sentiment analysis, 149, 151
Showrooming, 59
Social CRM, 51
Social media, 35, 39, 41, 67, 68
Social media pilots, 42
Stakeholder segment, 120
Statistical surveys, 162
Strategic targets, 116
Supplier governance, 8, 34, 255
Supplier management, 28

Tactical roadmap, 211
Technical performance
    assessment, 163

Training, 235
Transactional data, 37
Trend mining, 151

Unstructured data, 149, 151
Unstructured text data, 35
Usability testing, 144
User experience, 121

Value delivery, 228
Value propositions, 6, 74, 108,
    111, 118, 119, 120
Vendor relationship, 256, 258
Visual language, 106